HENRY PAOLUCCI
RICHARD C. CLARK

*PRESIDENTIAL POWER AND
CRISIS GOVERNMENT IN
THE AGE OF TERRORISM*

PREFACE BY ANNE PAOLUCCI
FOREWORD BY JACK RYAN

Library of Congress Cataloging in Processing Data

Paolucci, Henry.
    Presidential power and crisis government in the age of
terrorism / Henry Paolucci, Richard C. Clark; preface to
2003 edition by Anne Paolucci, foreword to 2003 edition by
Jack Ryan.
        p. cm.
    ISBN 1-932107-02-9 (alk. paper)
        1. Executive power—United States. 2. Legislative power—
United States. 3. Terrorism—Government policy—United
States. 4. War and emergency powers—United States. I. Clark,
Richard Charles. II. Title.
    JK516.P34 2003
    352.23'5'0973—dc21
                                    2002041647

Published for
THE BAGEHOT COUNCIL
by
GRIFFON HOUSE PUBLICATIONS
P. O. BOX 468
SMYRNA DE 19977
e-mail: *griffonhse@AOL.com*

CONTENTS

PREFACE

I was pleased but not altogether surprised when Griffon House Publications suggested we bring together in one volume the separate essays and book chapters which appear in this volume under the title *Presidential Power and Crisis Government in the Age of Terrorism.* The book is most timely, exploring in a number of well-documented writings, both the basic nature of constitutional government ("Part One" by Henry Paolucci) and the arguments relating to the restrictions necessary to protect the nation in times of crises ("Part Two" by Richard C. Clark).

What is extraordinary about this compilation is its *compelling* arguments and its *immediacy.* After decades of difficult negotiations and many attempts to find solutions to the ongoing mid-east crisis and the escalating terrorism it continues to encourage, the arguments presented in the pages that follow take on new meaning and force. Professor Paolucci, in his terse and precise account of the nature of government and the president's powers ("Part One"), provides us with a firm base from which we can venture into the dangerous area of how to deal with restrictions to those powers in national emergencies. Professor Clark, who has written at length on terrorism, gives us a well-documented account of why and how emergency presidential powers must be allowed ("Part Two"). His discussion is both theoretical and practical; his conclusions, clear and convincing.

Among the most striking passages in Professor Clark's discussion are Chapters 5 and 6 ("Prometheus Unbound" and "The Apollo Diversion"), where we are given — among other things — an in-depth account of the

cover-up connected with missing atomic materials at the
nuclear power plant in Apollo, Pennsylvania. The questions that surfaced at the time (we are reminded) have still
to be answered fully. And those answers, in turn, bear
directly on the present situation and the threat of world
terrorism. The Watergate affair pales by comparison.

Clark cites numerous authorities, on both sides, to
make his point. He brings back into the spotlight such
eminent (but today almost forgotten) statesmen like former
ambassador, John Davis Lodge, who warned in a recent
letter to the *New York Times* that we should discipline
ourselves to become "more geopolitical and less evangelical."

In his brief opening chapter of "Part One," "Presidential Prerogatives," Professor Paolucci recalls the
Watergate affair against a larger scenario which takes us
to the heart of the current subject, coming to focus on
Lincoln's insistence on saving the Union at all costs. His
second chapter, "The Political Pessimism of Our Founding
Fathers," is a terse reminder of the nature of government
as our early statesmen defined it, and as it has served us
for over two centuries. The third chapter — "The Exercise
of Sovereignty" — focuses on the book by that title written
by Charles Burton Marshall, who served for many years as
chief aide to Dean Acheson. Professor Paolucci touches
on several issues which have become much clearer with the
passage of time, including the dangers inherent in the
Atlantic Union resolution, which found support on both
sides of the Senate when it was introduced there but was
unanimously opposed by Young Americans for Freedom.
YAF's National Chairman at the time, Ronald F. Docksai,
expressed the dismay of the group when he wrote: "The
Atlantic Union resolution, as currently written, would, in
effect, lead to legal commitments made on behalf of the
United States government which we feel would compromise our legal and political sovereignty." (p. 24) Professor
Paolucci's short conclusion recalls the stakes involved in

presidential elections.

    Professor Paolucci and Professor Clark have both demonstrated their ability to deal with difficult matters that still plague us today, still demand resolution. The writings chosen for inclusion here are even more compelling today than at the time they first appeared, for the events which have taken place since then have made us more apprehensive, less certain of our safety as a people and a nation. It is a good time to review our case.

ANNE PAOLUCCI
New York
November 30, 2002

FOREWORD

In today's shaky and fearful environment of Islamic terrorist attacks at home, "suicide" bombers in the Middle-East, Chechen rebels in a Moscow cinema, sniper shootings in and near our nation's capital, and bombings of public buildings by outraged and misguided activists, citizens tend to fall into the trap of looking more and more to government to protect and defend them. While one of the principal functions of government is to do exactly that, in times of stress our legislators and administrators are often forced into imposing significantly greater infringement on personal liberty than would be permissible during normal times. The removal of legal restrictions on search and seizure, the ability to invade personal privacy through wiretapping and surveillance, the suspension of *habeas corpus* all can be made to appear necessary and acceptable to the man in the street when his family and life-style are threatened.

When Professors Paolucci and Clark wrote these articles, the crisis was the threat of atomic attack by our principal enemy. Security and accountability at nuclear energy plants within the U.S. was being criticized by the Government Accounting Office and the media. At the same time, racial and social unrest were plaguing our urban communities, our military forces were shunned and demoralized after a camouflaged defeat in Vietnam, and our federal government and President were pawns in the hands of avowed supra-nationalists who proclaimed the need for America — as the most powerful democracy on the earth — to sacrifice its own national sovereignty in the hope of a permanent world peace.

That did not happen. Our sovereignty was not compromised, nor was presidential authority undermined, even in those critical times. On the other hand, as Professor Paolucci points out in Part I of this book, President Nixon could not have been justified in the use of strong presidential prerogatives for the Watergate affair, or in his claim that the "Pentagon Papers" stolen by Daniel Elsberg and published by the *New York Times* were in any way affecting our national security. Attempts at the misuse of Presidential power under the guise of national security have indeed been rare in our short history. President Lincoln's admonition during the Civil War — that the Constitution or provisions thereof may be wisely sacrificed to preserve the people, but never the people sacrificed to preserve the Constitution itself, or any other such document — remains a sober warning as to where the line should be drawn. Lincoln saved the Union with his fierce insistence on the hard necessities of legitimate government. No such argument can serve in Nixon's case.

Commenting over a hundred years ago on our American political system, the English economist and historian, Walter Bagehot, noted that government by discussion as it existed in Parliament was better able to meet emergencies than the American system because of the speed with which the the Prime Minister and his Cabinet could be changed. That, he said, gave the English system some of the advantages of dictatorial efficiency. The American system had no such advantages. Still, the American people, if not their Constitution, Bagehot acknowledged, had seemed to manage anyway, in times of crisis.

Frederick M. Watkins, a professor of politics and government at Yale University during the 1930s, whose thoughts on the subject of crisis government are discussed in these pages, perhaps phrased it best for our time. Writing about the idea of "emergency powers" and whether or not temporary dictatorship can be made to serve the ends of constitutional government, he posed the question of what a nation that is faced with an immediate threat to its existence could afford to calculate in terms of a very distant future: "There is no point," he wrote, "in worrying about the future unless you are sure that you have a future to worry about."

But it was George Washington who first gave eloquent expression to the political imperative to preserve the nation at all costs, exhorting "we the people" to protect our union and our national sovereignty:

> It is of infinite moment that you should properly estimate the immense value of our national union to your collective and individual happiness; that you should cherish a cordial, habitual, and immovable attachment to it; accustoming yourselves to think and speak of it as of the palladium of your political safety and prosperity; watching over its preservation with jealous anxiety; discountenancing whatever may suggest even a suspicion that it can in any event be abandoned. (September 17, 1796)

That early admonition is the burden of this book. In Part I Henry Paolucci provides a solid discussion on the president's powers and the nature of government. In Part II, Richard C. Clark — who is well informed on how crippled constitutions can be reformed to withstand revolutionary subversion — discusses crisis government and the danger of nuclear terrorism in that context, reminding us of the mysteries of missing or unaccounted-for uranium at our atomic energy plants, as well as a variety of other diversions, smugglings, and hijackings of nuclear materials. In the concluding chapter, Professor Paolucci returns to remind us how a close presidential election can offer leverage to special interest groups to further their private agendas, but also how important *national* interests must overshadow commitments made during a campaign.

The danger to our national security is greater today than it was three decades ago, when these pages were written. Yet, despite the time elapsed since they first appeared, the arguments expressed in them have lost none of their immediacy. They are just as compelling and perhaps even more relevant today, when the difficulties of insuring for all nations a "separate and equal station" threaten to escalate into increasingly devastating terrorist attacks and world-wide conflicts.

JACK RYAN
The Bagehot Council
December 12, 2002

PART ONE
(HENRY PAOLUCCI)

THE NATURE OF GOVERNMENT AND PRESIDENTIAL POWER

1. PRESIDENTIAL PREROGATIVES

Inscribed on the back wall of the Lincoln Memorial in Washington are these fateful words: "In this temple, as in the hearts of the people for whom he saved the Union, the memory of Abraham Lincoln is enshrined forever."

Lincoln's temple is the crown of a mighty cross in our nation's capital — a cross that has Capitol Hill at its base and the White House and Jefferson Memorial at the ends of its cross beam. Washington's Monument, rising near the intersection of the long and short beams, is like a spear in the side of an invisible saviour of our body politic, for whose sacrificial agony the Lincoln Memorial, with all its solemn words, will one day serve as a crown of glory.

Washington, Jefferson, Lincoln — each confirmed in word and deed that profoundest truth of our Western political tradition, which is that coercive government is at best a necessary evil, and that when free men deny either its evil or its necessity, they soon cease to be free.

The Watergate affair recalls our attention to that painful truth, but unfortunately with misplaced emphasis and miscast spokesmen. To the delight of the Ervins and Weickers, John Mitchell put the brand of White House "horrors" on what officious John Ehrlichman professed to defend as presidential prerogatives for national security.

Mr. Ehrlichman was a poor advocate. To save himself with his old boss, he made a cynically ruthless appeal to *raison d'etat*: a principle of statecraft for which, it has been alleged, the Anglo-American heirs of the Cromwells don't have so much as an equivalent term, much less the awful thing itself — even though Winston Churchill summed it up quite aptly when, to justify the Anglo-Soviet alliance against Hitler, he snarled: "Madam, I would make a friend

3

of the devil himself if it would save England."

But the principle of *raison d'etat* is ill applied in Mr.
Nixon's case. By committing his administration to pursue
peace as an end in itself, our President abandoned the
grounds on which presidential prerogatives ultimately rest.
In its Preamble, our Constitution prescribes six ends that
We the People of the United States are pledged to prefer
to peace. Yet President Nixon, guided by Henry Kissinger,
presumed to re-order those prescribed priorities. Fearful
of the responsibilities of defense in the nuclear age, he
succumbed to the spurious argument that preservation of
our nation's sovereign independence can no longer be – as
it was in the days of Washington, Jefferson, and Lincoln, to
say nothing of Wilson and FDR – its highest law.

What about the Nixon administration's case against
Daniel Ellsberg? Was it a "national security" prosecution in
the traditional sense? Senator Sam Ervin, a staunch de-
fender of our nation's sovereignty against the supra-na-
tionalist pretensions of the so-called Genocide Convention, correctly rejected the notion. Ellsberg was charged,
he noted, not with giving treacherous aid and comfort to
enemy leaders whom the inscrutable Mr. Kissinger courted
for years, but merely with "stealing some papers that
belonged to the government."

On this same point, presidential spokesman John
T. Lofton tried to "set the record straight" in the August
1973 issue of *First Monday*, insisting that Mr. Nixon had no
motive for political vindictiveness against Ellsberg, "since
the Kennedy and Johnson Administrations were hurt by
the disclosures." It is no secret, of course, that the Pentagon Papers served to enhance President Nixon's claim that
he, rather than Johnson or Kennedy, deserved to be
honoured by the Harvard-MIT "conscience elite" as the
first American President of the Atomic Age to be "thoroughly committed to peace."

But why then did so many presumably anti-Nixon
academicians and journalists collaborate to get the pro-

Nixon Pentagon Papers published? Mr. Lofton's explanation reads: "It is evident that the liberal media had, by 1971, written off the Kennedy-Johnson Vietnam policy as a disaster. If, in order to save high-priority liberal fantasies about Vietnam, they had to destroy some liberal myths about Kennedy and Johnson, the liberal media were ready." That statement also helps to explain why the cases against the *Times* and Elisberg were so ineptly argued. The Nixon administration was not about to go to court to injure itself!

Where did Mr. Nixon really stand on presidential prerogatives? Was he prepared to defend even so shabby a version of *raison d'etat* as Ehrlichman advanced? Hardly. With Watergate, as with Kissinger's peace strategy and Moynihan's welfare reforms, he apparently intended to pursue a Disraelian course, hoping to "dish" the opposition by claiming its positions as his own. Out-Weickering Senator Weicker, he thus humbly protested on August 15: "If we lose our liberties, we will have little use for security. Instances have come to light where zeal for security did go too far. . . ."

The lesson of Watergate for Nixon appeared to be that while he could "dish" the liberals all he wanted with *détentes* and conditional surrenders abroad, and with Moynihan reforms at home, he could never again dream of threatening them with secret reserves of "conservative" Mitchells, Haldemans, and Ehrlichmans. Such reserves are herewith to be committed to the flames — or rather, to the muck of Watergate- — forever. Emerson must have had a prescient vision of our crippled post-Watergate presidency in mind when he wrote in "Compensation": "The President has paid dear for his White House . . . . To preserve for a short time so conspicuous an appearance before the world, he is content to eat dust before the real powers behind the throne."

2. THE POLITICAL PESSIMISM OF OUR FOUNDING FATHERS

The *Constitution of the United States* is the world's great masterpiece of political pessimism. The men who framed it were realists about human nature. Having just come out of a bloody revolution in which most of them had fought against and killed cousins, friends, and even brothers for the sake of political liberty, they could not delude themselves about the hard realities of political government. They did not presume to commit themselves or their posterity to pursue peace at all costs, or to abolish poverty at all costs, or to root out once and forever all ignorance, treachery, violence, personal arrogance, factional selfishness, bigotry, greed, envy, hatred, cruelty, luxury, insolence, impudence, calumnies, plots, plunderings, rapes, murders, or the innumerable other evils "that do not," as St. Augustine long ago expressed it, "easily come to mind but that never absent themselves from the actuality of human existence."

The political pessimism of our founding fathers had deep roots. They were master-students of the great political theorists of the Western tradition, most of whom, from Plato, Aristotle, and Polybius, to Machiavelli, Hobbes, and Montesquieu, were avowed pessimists; and they knew that even the professed optimists of that tradition — the Ciceros, Lockes, and Rousseaus — had at the heart of their doctrine a realism about the prerogative powers of political self-defense which, when we finally discern it, rivets our attention with the compelling force of a Medusa's head.

But the pessimism of the framers of our Constitution also had religious roots. According to the Gospels, Jesus Christ was unmistakably a political pessimist. He did not pretend that earthly states could survive without an organized willingness to restrain domestic law-breakers and to wage war. He taught that poverty could never be completely eliminated by human provision and rejected as utterly vain the age-old expectation that the world's wise men would one day succeed, through their collective wisdom, in transforming this vale of tears into a regime of genuine happiness for all mankind.

In the tradition that brought the *New Testament* teachings down to our Founding Fathers, the most important political lesson was, without question, the one that emerges from Pilate's interrogation of Jesus in the Gospel according to St. John. When the Founder of Christianity was arrested on the charge that, like the American Black Muslims, he was planning to set up an independent state within the territorial jurisdiction of another state, the local Roman governor pointedly asked him what he thought of the traditional prerogatives of political sovereignty. And the answers Jesus gave were frank and unequivocal — quite unlike those we are used to hearing from the radical-chic advocates of civil disobedience and "creative disorder" today.

"Knowest though not," Pilate asked Jesus, "that I have power to crucify you, and have power to release you?" In response, Jesus affirmed that such powers as the governor claimed over persons brought before the bar were legitimately his and were, indeed, God-given. "Thou couldst have no power at all against me," he answered, "except it were given you from above." Pressed to say whether he actually claimed to be an independent king within the Roman jurisdiction, again Jesus didn't mince words. He did not for a moment deny his Messianic Kingship. Rather, he denied only that he had ever claimed to be a king of the Jews in an earthly Zionist sense. "My kingdom," Jesus assured Pilate, "is not of this world." And then he went on to indicate how basic and unalienable, in his judgment, is the right of an earthly state to wage war to prevent its subjugation by foreign or alien will. "If my kingdom were of this world," said Jesus, "then would my servants fight that I should not be delivered to the Jews."

There is surely a powerful truth of political pessimism in that response. Those words of the Gospel tell us that, if Jesus Christ himself, the Prince of Peace, were President of the United States, he would flatly reject, out of hand, the professed "pacifism" of the Nixon Administration. Even as the Founder of Christianity drove the money-changers out of the temple for trading on sacred things, so would he drive out of the government of our earthly kingdom all the self-righteous McGeorge Bundys, Walt Rostows, and Henry Kissingers who urged our Presidents to make a public sacrifice of the sovereign earthly foundations of our Republic. Jesus says that if his kingdom were of this world his servants would fight even against his fellow Jews, if they sought to subjugate him. But our Harvard-MIT presidential advisers for national security affairs tell us instead that it is time we gave up the right to fight; and that, since that right is "the root of national sovereignty," it is now actually "an American interest to see an end to nationhood as it has been historically defined." That our Presidents should endure such counsellors by their side is the great public scandal of our time. It has deprived our government of effective leadership, thereby creating a power vacuum in the world which must sooner or later be filled by earthly rulers whose "servants" are not committed to preserving peace at all costs.

Because he was the Heavenly Christ, Jesus denied that Jews who became Christians could rightly form a state of their own in this world. Sovereign statehood could remain an expectation of Jews only in the measure that they declined to accept Jesus as the long-awaited Messiah. Jews as Christians were urged by Jesus to pledge allegiance to whatever states they happened to inhabit. He urged them to pay their taxes willingly and to render unto temporal rulers what the law prescribes, even when, as was often the case, those rulers pursued domestic and foreign policies which ran counter to traditional Jewish interests. St. Peter and St. Paul, who considered themselves loyal Jews, fully shared the worldly political pessimism of their Master; and through them his doctrine passed to the Church Fathers, the greatest of whom — St. Augustine of Africa — traced out all its implications in a rounded theory of politics that was destined to dominate Christian thinking for over a thousand years. The Protestant Reformers, Luther and Calvin, no less than St. Thomas Aquinas, were heirs of the Augustinian legacy; and it was their immediate disciples who gave that unflinchingly realistic doctrine the modern relevance with which it is expressed in the writings of Hobbes, Locke, and Burke, as also in the authors of the *American Federalist Papers*.

Surely St. Peter and St. Paul would have felt themselves at home in the political doctrine of our *Federalist Papers*. For those papers are saturated with the realistic conviction that political government is at best a necessary evil. It is necessary because greater evils would be unleashed without it: because, apart from its legal, customary, and educational restraints, men tend to behave worse than the wildest beasts, perverting even reason itself (which is God's image in man) to gratify their most vicious appetites. And it remains evil all the while because, even when it functions most effectively, it can do so only by placing certain human beings in offices of concentrated power which can readily be abused. Power by its very nature tends to corrupt; but the worst of it is that, in the spheres of criminal justice and foreign relations, the necessities of government actually oblige persons in positions of highest trust to commit, for the common good, acts of the very kind that civilizing society, with its laws and education, attempt to repress in the conduct of the mass of its members.

In *Federalist Paper* No.51, where he argued simultaneously for a concentration of powers to preserve the

Union and for a separation of powers to guard against
domestic tyranny, James Madison wrote: "Ambition must
be made to counteract ambition." And on that principle of
political realism he proceeded to erect his renowned defense of our constitutional system of checks and balances.
"It may be a reflection on human nature," he explained,
"that such devices should be necessary to control the
abuses of government. But what is government itself, but
the greatest of all reflections on human nature?" Then
come these momentous words, the pessimistic sense of
which might well have been drawn straight out of the
Gospels, St. Paul, and St. Augustine:

> If men were angels, no government would be necessary.
> If angels were to govern men, neither external nor
> internal controls on government would be necessary. In
> framing a government which is to be administered by
> men over men, the great difficulty lies in this: you must
> first enable the government to control the governed; and
> in the next place oblige it to control itself. A dependence
> on the people is, no doubt, the primary control on the
> government; but experience has taught mankind the
> necessity of auxiliary precautions.

Madison, Alexander Hamilton, John Jay, authors of
the *Federalist Papers*, were all of a mind that the first
necessity of legitimate government is to provide for the
common defense. As to the industrial and military power
that would have to be concentrated in government to meet
that necessity, Hamilton had urged that no limit could
reasonably be prescribed. Authority

> to raise armies; to build and equip fleets; to prescribe
> rules for the government of both; to direct their opera-
> tions; to provide for their support . . . ought to exist
> without limitation, because it is impossible to foresee or
> to define the extent and variety of national exigencies
> and the correspondent extent and variety of the means
> which may be necessary to satisfy them. The circum-
> stances that endanger the safety of nations are infinite,

and for this reason no constitutional shackles can wisely be imposed on the power to which the care of it is committed.

That sums up the dilemma of all free government. Power must be concentrated for defense, but divided, checked, and balanced, to prevent its abusive application to purposes other than defense. How that dilemma is to be resolved in practice President Lincoln demonstrated by his conduct during the Civil War, when his powers were very nearly absolute. Speaking for the Abolitionists, Horace Greeley asked him at one point to use all his powers to put an end to slavery at all costs; to which Lincoln replied by distinguishing sharply between his unlimited prerogative powers to preserve the union and his checked and balanced powers to pursue his personal "ideals." In his letter to Greeley he says:

> My paramount object in this struggle *is* to save the Union and is *not* to save or destroy slavery . . . . What I do about slavery and the colored race, I do because I believe it helps to save the Union; and what I forbear, I forbear because I do *not* believe it would help save the Union . . . . I have here stated my purpose according to my view of *official* duty, and I intend no modification of my oft-expressed *personal* wish that all men, everywhere, could be free.

How removed from that spirit of Lincoln is our governmental leadership today! Our most recent Presidents have let themselves be bullied intellectually into preaching that our political priorities have now to be radically reordered. From now on our government is to have unlimited powers to abolish poverty, bigotry, pollution, social inequality, racial prejudice, ignorance, discrimination against homosexuals, criminals, traitors, etc., etc., and no powers at all to raise armies and fight to prevent our subjugation to an alien dominated government.

Soon, if we continue along this path, every other

people in the world will be armed to the teeth and ready to fight (as even Ghandi's "pacifists" have lately proved), while we are left to sink deeper and deeper into slothful indecision. No wonder our domestic minorities are looking for non-American "ideals" to animate their spirits! While our alienated intellectuals persist in denying us an image of America that deserves to be loved by all who call themselves citizens, our Blacks seek desperately for a sense of patriotic community by calling one another brothers and sisters. Our Spanish-speaking immigrants, and now our Chinese also, are looking elsewhere, more and more, for the inspirations of patriotism. It is virtually the same with all our minorities, not excluding even the American Jews, who were the first of the non-WASP groups to really "make it" in America. Many of our Jews are rapidly experiencing almost total political alienation, even though they rank exceptionally high in numbers among the wealthier classes and share an absolute monopoly (according to Father Andrew M. Greeley, *New York Times Magazine*, Sept. 12, 1971) with WASPs in the top professorial posts of our most prestigious universities.

Many of us earnestly believe that if the American Jewish community were to reject the anti-nationalist, anti-military bias that now prevails in our universities, it could do more than any other distinguishable group, at this time, to set this country right. American Jews as a group have the necessary economic power and they also enjoy an unprecedentedly strong intellectual leadership. But with the general current of liberal thought still running steadily in the opposite direction, it is understandable that Jews should have been reluctant to buck it. Their best energies have gone, instead, into promoting the U.N., into building bridges of "peace" between the superpowers, and even into providing — with the Israeli religious *kibbutz* — a distinctively Jewish alternative to Godless Marxism.

Karl Marx was, of course, a political optimist. Unlike Jesus Christ, or St. Paul, or our Founding Fathers, he believed that the major evils that have traditionally plagued mankind could be eliminated — that a final, earthly solution to all our difficulties was not only possible but indeed inevitable. All it would require, he believed, was a concentration of coercive power in the right hands: the hands of tightly disciplined cadres of tough revolutionaries. Aided by liberal fellow-travellers, such revolutionaries would first overthrow, one by one, all existing governments; and then they would proceed to annihilate, if need be, all classes of people who might in any way offer resistance to the inauguration of their ideal stateless, classless world community.

But Adolph Hitler too — we must never forget — was an advocate of *final solutions*. And he took his lead straight out of the *Communist Manifesto*, modifying Marx's scheme only in the very central detail of identifying the Jews (rather than the Gentile capitalists) as the chief obstacles to universal happiness. Hitler accused the Jews of being Pluto-Socialists, by which he meant that they were both vicious capitalists and vicious agitators of the lower classes. His proposed "final solution" consisted in freeing both labor and capital from Jewish leadership so that both could be united in the greater Germany, which was destined, in his judgment, to rule the entire world, without restraints, for a thousand years.

After Hitler's defeat in World War II, the Western liberals finally came forward with their own long-range design for a *final solution*: the United Nations Organization, which they hoped would gradually concentrate in itself sufficient power to enforce a universal peace for all mankind. With Hitler destroyed, and with America having no final, optimistic solution of its own to offer, their idea was to present the U.N. as the one rational alternative to the Marxist design for universal peace. Internationalists the world over flocked to the new colors.

Typical of U.N. advocates in the early days was Richard Crossman, Labor Party Member of Parliament in

Britain and long-time leading spokesman of the English Fabian Socialists. In 1948 he wrote a powerful plea for the U.N., in which he played ruthlessly on Jewish fears to gain his point. With millions of Jews sealed up in the Soviet Union, and many millions more prospering in the United States, Crossman hoped to use Jewish fears of a Soviet-American conflict to strengthen his pro-U.N. argument. With extraordinary brazenness, he wrote (*Palestine Mission*, New York, 1947, p.205):

> World Jewry can survive only in a world of decency and toleration; it would be submerged in a Russian-American conflict for world mastery. For in the next total and atomic war . . . the communist and the anti-communist ideologies would be ruthlessly opposed, in all their irrationality, until in the last resort, victor and vanquished would be merely the incarnation of a stronger and a weaker concentration of brute force . . . . The fate of World Jewry and of the British Commonwealth alike is bound up with the success or failure of the United Nations . . . . "One World," neither communist, nor anticommunist, neither American nor Russian, is the condition of their survival.

But after all we have seen at the U.N. — dancing, fist fights, expulsions of original members, and obvious maneuverings to expel even Israel itself — who in his right mind could conceivably expect any self-respecting people to entrust their ultimate fate to its care? Despite Crossman, World Jewry now quite obviously looks to itself, rather than to the U.N., for an alternative to Marx. The great Israeli philosopher Martin Buber has spoken frankly on the subject. Back in 1950 he was already arguing that not only the Jews but all mankind would have to choose ultimately between Moscow and Jerusalem. Those two names symbolized for Buber two forms of socialism, one Godless, the other God-centered, each offering mankind a universal "kingdom of this world." In his own words: "The essential point is to decide on the fundamentals: a restructuring of society as a league of leagues . . . or a devouring of an amorphous society by the omnipotent state — socialist pluralism or so-called socialist unitarianism . . . . We must designate one of the two poles between which our choice lies by the formidable name of 'Moscow.' The other I would make bold to call 'Jerusalem'." (*Martin Buber*, ed. by Will Herberg, New York, 1956, p. 141)

We are back, apparently, where we were in the days when Jesus Christ talked with Pilate about the prerogatives of political sovereignty. Unless we can draw strength from our roots once more, we shall have to learn all over again, by trial and error, the lessons of two thousand years of Western experience with political liberty.

But we need not fail. Jews, Christians, Muslims, and loyal secularists alike can re-dedicate ourselves to making this Commonwealth of civilized tolerance work. Our Founding Fathers who did not mistake themselves for angels or saints, have built well for us. To secure the independence of our sovereign union of sovereign states they gladly pledged to each other their lives, their fortunes, and their sacred honor. Let us, in turn, commit ourselves, as loyal citizens and heirs, to do the same.

3. THE EXERCISE OF SOVEREIGNTY

The Exercise of Sovereignty is the title of a very important book by Charles Burton Marshall, who used to be a top foreign policy advisor in the days when tough Harry Truman was President and Richard M. Nixon was calling for a new Crusade in Europe to free captive nations from the communist tyranny. This collection of papers on foreign policy, stressing the meaning of sovereignty, was first published in 1965, by The Johns Hopkins Press, Baltimore, Maryland. But its arguments became electrifyingly important today, while Mr. Nixon — captive of the internationalist intelligentsia — cements his trade and disarmament deals with Brezhnev and lets the enemies of our nationhood at home bury our Presidency in the muck and mire of Watergate.

In an earlier book, *The Limits of Foreign Policy* (Johns Hopkins, 1954), Marshall had warned against the coming assault on our sovereignty by writing: "In the current phase of international affairs the reigning clichés and formulas reflect an obsession to discount national individuality. Rare is the statesman who does not have a plan for some other nations, if not also his own, to pool something or other and to act as if they were one instead of several." Adding an after-word for a new edition in 1968, Marshall asked his readers to ponder, while the internationalists prated about a created world order, "Whether a nation should entertain ideas about order in the world while losing will and talent for keeping order in the streets."

In that same after-word of 1968, Marshall further warned:

It is improvident to count on any pacificatory formula premised on another government's willingness to extinguish itself. It is prudent to recognize every other government, even the friendliest, as in some degree a competitor and therefore not to count on its support on any other basis than its own self interest. It is wise to keep in mind the elements of discontinuity affecting states and to be reconciled to the impermanence of even so-called permanent engagements with others.

But doesn't the best hope for mankind lie in promoting international understanding by having summit meetings where old enemies drink toasts to peace? Marshall replies by citing "Indians and Pakistanis, Arabs and Israelis, Poles and Germans as paired examples of peoples given to understanding each other only too well."

But Marshall's *The Exercise of Sovereignty* takes us at once to the heart of our nation's present dilemma, where Presidents are advised on matters of ultimate national security by Bundys, Rostows, and Kissingers who believe, with the international communists, that the nation-state system is doomed to perish, and that, in Rostow's words, it is now a legitimate American "interest to see an end to nationhood as it has been historically defined."

Marshall published his book just when Walt Rostow was replacing McGeorge Bundy as White House Special Assistant for National Security Affairs. Most of the Kennedy people were then in league to try to keep Lyndon Johnson from wrecking their Vietnam no-win war plans by exercising his sovereign prerogatives as President. A newspaper headline — "Sovereignty Outmoded, says Rusk" — serves Marshall as a point of departure. That phrase, he explains, was often thrown up at him, when he talked to academic audiences, as if it were a formula for solving the world's problems. When questioned about the "obsolescence" of sovereignty, Marshall usually answered by outlining some of the political characteristics of sovereignty and then asking which ones precisely the questioner wanted to eliminate.

"In the general case," Marshall writes, "it turns out

that my questioner finds national responsibility awesome,
risky, and expensive. Sovereignty to him epitomizes the
risks and burdens and by getting rid of the concept or the
word he hopes to alleviate them."

Marshall then goes on to define with considerable
care the attributes of sovereignty. His terms are not academic abstraction. Marshall served many years as a naval
officer and had long professional experience in "committee chambers on Capitol Hill, secret councils of the State
Department, active practice in foreign missions," and crisis
service under Dean Acheson, before he joined the faculty
at the Johns Hopkins School of Advanced International
Studies. His characterization of the main attributes of
sovereignty is a statesman's characterization, made for free
citizens of a self-governing Republic. "Sovereignty," writes
Marshall,

> entails having a scheme of authority — a ruling group —
> capable of maintaining dependable social order perva-
> sively over a demarcated area. Sovereignty entails com-
> mand of the allegiance of a determining portion of the
> persons and groups encompassed in that area. Sover-
> eignty entails having a common set of recollections from
> the past and expectations for the future forming a
> pattern of identity among such persons and groups.
>
> Sovereignty entails a conscious general purpose to
> amount to something significant in the world's annals.
> Sovereignty entails a capacity and a will to command
> means and to devote them to give effect to common
> preferences. Sovereignty involves a capacity to enter
> into and effectuate obligations. Sovereignty involves
> capacity to effect environing conditions as well as to be
> affected by them. Sovereignty requires having some
> system of agency capable of representing the realm in
> external dealings — able to communicate authentically
> and conclusively on its behalf to others beyond the span
> of jurisdiction.

This enumeration of characteristics outlines what

must be the status of every sovereign state of this earth worthy of the name. If the Soviet Union, Red China, Israel, or any other power is to realize its purposes in relations with any other powers, it must make use of these characteristics of sovereignty. Could the United States hope to remain "secure" as a nation without them? Marshall writes:

> I would wish my own society to prize, to hold on to, and go on cultivating every one of these faculties and attributes. It would forfeit anyone of them at its peril.

What about Rostow's idea (which is also Kissinger's idea) of the urgency of transcending our national sovereignty and Rusk's talk of its obsolescence? Marshall responds with a magisterial rebuke, writing:

> The notion of solving great problems through planned obsolescence of sovereignty is simply one of those airy generalizations abundant in discussions of international relations — something handy to say before an assemblage but not of much account in engaging in actualities. The perils and perplexities in the world about us rise not so much from an excess of the constituent qualities of sovereignty in the entities passing as nation-states, as from an entirely opposite circumstance. A great many of them have not achieved those qualities. Realizing them may be beyond the ultimate capabilities of some.

Marshall knows that the idea of solving the world's problems by phasing out sovereignty, with the United States showing the way, to be immediately followed by the Soviet Union, is all-pervasive in our universities. Advocates of that idea swarmed into Washington in 1961 to advise our President on national security affairs. After Kennedy's assassination, they clung to office under President Johnson, whom they despised, but only to help "dump" him in the end. Henry Kissinger is at it now, walking a tightrope to get us on an irreversible course of submissive detente with the communist powers while the authority of our Presidency is lost perhaps beyond recovery because of "national security" counterespionage capers in which our top national security advisor may have had a guiding hand.

Does Mr. Nixon, with Kissinger constantly at his ear, know that his chief duty as President is to exercise the sovereignty vested in our government to enable it to preserve our national union at all costs? Or is he too deeply infected with the notion — the Bundy, Rostow, Kissinger notion — that the time has come for the United States to surrender its sovereignty to purchase peace in the nuclear age?

Mr. Nixon's oath of office forbids him to entertain such a notion. And yet, when congressional champions of the so-called Atlantic Union — which is a scheme for surrender of sovereignty — approached him in March of 1973, he gave his emphatic support. Watergate was on his heels, and so he looked eagerly to the left for salvation, thereby proving that there are things much worse than a Watergate cover-up that a President may dare to undertake when he travels down a mistaken path.

On March 10, 1973, President Nixon wrote a letter to Representative Paul Findley of Illinois who cited it in the Congressional Record of March 15 under the heading: "President Nixon Endorses Atlantic Union." The President's letter reads:

> Dear Paul: It was good to see you on March 2 and have an opportunity to discuss the Atlantic Union resolution and other legislative matters. As a goal and concept I have favored Atlantic Union for many years, dating back to my service in Congress. As President I have made it a policy not to give specific endorsement to resolutions of this kind, but I want you to know that my long-standing position on the concept and the goal which you are seeking to achieve through this resolution has not changed. With best wishes always, sincerely, Richard Nixon.

In his Congressional Record comments, Representative Findley explained:

> Never before has a President of the United States pub-

licly stated his support for Atlantic Union as a means of dealing with the supranational problems which confront us . . . . While President Nixon's letter did not endorse specific language on Atlantic Union, he assured me personally when I discussed the question with him in the Oval Office of the White House on March 2 that he will sign the resolution if it is passed by Congress.

What is the proposed Atlantic Union? In reintroducing his resolution for it in January 1973, Rep. Findley said:

> The resolution contemplates a massive advance in political institutions, one that indeed would be historic . . . . The nations of the world have developed the capability to destroy one another completely, but we have yet to build a political system that can prevent a nuclear holocaust . . . a political institution large enough to deal successfully with the supranational problems that now confront us . . . . Social phenomena, such as the youth culture, are no respectors of the nation-state . . . . The problems are already supranational. It is up [to us] to develop the supranational institutions to deal adequately with them.

That resolution passed, without a single protesting vote, in a Senate where Barry Goldwater, John Tower , and James L. Buckley sit. Senator Goldwater has lately been very glum about the future of the Republican Party. In a discussion with Dan Rather of CBS, on the anniversary of the Watergate break-in, Goldwater said:

> The thing that bothers me is, here I have spent over a third of my life, trying to build the Republican party, adding my little bit to it, having been successful in the South and in the Southwest, and then all of a sudden, as I near the end of my time in politics, I wonder — what the hell's it all been for? Here we are just drifting around . . . . I feel terribly let down . . . . I get up in the mornings and I think, oh, what the hell, what can you do?

Sen. Goldwater has worked hard for his party and feels let down after Watergate. But what about his posture

on the anti-nationalist Atlantic Union project? In his March
18 remarks on the resolution, Rep. Findley ended boast-
fully:

> The Atlantic Union resolution, which has earned the
> support of political figures ranking from former Sen.
> Eugene J. McCarthy (D-Minn) to President Nixon and
> from Gov. Nelson A. Rockefeller of New York to Sen.
> Barry M. Goldwater (R-Ariz), opens doors the free world
> can ill afford to see remain closed.

Those doors are wide open now. In *The Atlantic
Union Bulletin* of May, 1973, the opening editorial reads:
"Dr. Henry Kissinger's April 23 speech calling for a new
'Atlantic Charter' makes the reconsideration of the Atlantic Union Resolution in the U.S. House of Representatives
more possible." And the *Bulletin* explains at length why
Kissinger's "gradualist" approach is best. That was, of
course, proved in the no-win Vietnam war, where Kissinger
"got us out" without a right-wing backlash. And such
gradualism has cost us — since Mr. Nixon took over in 1969
— a mere 20,000 Americans killed and 150,000 wounded!

Such gradualism in surrendering American lives,
honor, and sovereignty is the great American scandal of
our time, for which the Watergate cover-up is itself but a
cover-up. Gradualism toward world government — that's
the Atlantic Union scheme as Clarence Streit and his old
and new friends originally conceived it. In Mr. Streit's
words:

> It [contains] only the germ of world government . . . . It
> recognizes world government only as an eventual, ulti-
> mate goal . . . extending its federal relationship to others.

In the same gradualist vein, Rep. Findley wrote to
President Nixon:

> Your support of the resolution would be the kind of
> pragmatic step which you have made clear is your pre-
> ferred policy for attaining great goals . . . . Small prag-
> matic steps are easier to take if they are known to be
> down the path to a clear goal.

Unlike Senators Goldwater, Tower, Thurmond, and Buckley, Young Americans for Freedom has repeatedly voiced its opposition to the Atlantic Union drive, which is now targeted on the youth of America. A recent counter-resolution passed unanimously by the YAF National Board of Directors read in part:

Whereas the concept of the Atlantic Union is entirely alien to the founding principles of Young Americans for Freedom as outlined in the Sharon Statement: more specifically it is in conflict with the clause which states "We will be free only so long as the national sovereignty of the United States is secure," and . . . whereas the Atlantic Union represents the first step toward World Government and threatens the survival of the United States as a free and independent Republic, . . . be it hereby resolved, by the National Board of Directors of Young Americans for Freedom that we are unalterably opposed to any effort by the United States to develop an Atlantic Federal Union either within or without the framework of the United Nations.

Richard A. Delgaudio of New York YAF introduced that anti-Atlantic Union resolution that was unanimously passed, and YAF's National Chairman, Ronald Docksai, summed up its argument most pointedly in a recent letter to a critic:

The Atlantic Union resolution, as currently written, would, in effect, lead to legal commitments made on behalf of the United States government which we feel would compromise our legal and political sovereignty. This is why many conservatives on Capitol Hill, including Democrats such as Mario Biaggi, have worked against this measure. They see it as the legal relative of the Genocide Treaty . . . . It is impossible for YAF to remain silent on an issue which, the National Board feels, *seriously* threatens our political sovereignty.

Congressman Biaggi of New York had originally co-sponsored the Atlantic Union Resolution in the House. But after he had explored the matter in depth, he saw where the "small pragmatic step" was leading and therefore testified before the House Foreign Affairs Subcommittee on International Organizations and Movements:

> Mr. Chairman . . . . I wish publicly to state that I no longer support this proposal . . . [which], if pursued, could lead to a loss of national sovereignty for the United States. While I believe fully that we must promote international cooperation . . . I do not believe that such cooperation must come at the cost of losing control over our destiny as a Nation. Yet it appears that that is exactly where we are headed with this proposal.

A similar disavowal from Congressman Peter A. Peyser of New York is also on record. Would there were more. The President needs such pressure from the right. But perhaps it is too late in Mr. Nixon's case. Perhaps his Harvard-MIT internationalist advisors, led by Kissinger, have already talked Poor Richard into vying for the distinction of being the last President of the United States. What price Watergate!

We know why our professed enemies abroad and at home want us to give up our sovereign nationhood. But what seduces so many others, not only in the universities, but also in our government, to lend their support to the gradualist, pragmatic, one little step at a time approach to national suicide? We know there is a communist open conspiracy to build its world tyranny on the ruins of our nation-state system. We know there is an open conspiracy of American academicians to prevent a nuclear holocaust *at all costs* by similar means. But what seduces our ordinary, civic minded, even conservative senators to blind themselves to the ultimate peril for this nation in all this talk of supranational political solutions to the world's problems?

Professor Marshall's *The Exercise of Sovereignty* is a thoroughly sober, calmly reasoned answer. He knows the ultimate domestic source of the tragic impulse of our time which has virtually paralyzed our governing class. There are tougher books on the subject: *Will America Surrender?*,

by S. M. Draskovich, is another such book. The most
powerful indictment of the sickness of our ruling class
available in print today is, I dare say, *Our Dispossessed
Majority*, by Wilmot Robertson.

PART TWO
(RICHARD C. CLARK)

CRISIS GOVERNMENT AND TERRORISM

4. CRISIS GOVERNMENT

Lincoln vs. Ervin

During the Watergate Hearings in the summer of 1973, Sam Ervin, the Senate's learned constitutional expert, emotionally announced to all the nation that the greatest constitutional decision ever handed down by the Supreme Court was *Ex parte* Milligan. According to Senator Ervin, at issue in the Milligan case was whether President Lincoln's "underlings" (as Ervin evasively termed it) could suspend certain fundamental constitutional rights during a time of great crisis. But it was Lincoln himself, not any underlings, who argued cogently and at length that the Constitution or provisions thereof may be wisely sacrificed to preserve the people, but never the people sacrificed to preserve the Constitution or any other document.

A wealth of additional evidence, from Lincoln (not his underlings), might have been presented. Without belaboring the point, we add just this one other decisive statement by our Civil War President:

> Are all the laws *but one* to go unexecuted, and the Government itself go to pieces lest that one be violated? Even in such a case, would not the official oath be broken if the Government should be overthrown when it was believed that disregarding the single law would tend to preserve it?

Lincoln's extraordinary amplification of "war powers" in the interest of preserving the nation was subsequently challenged on several grounds, including the argument that Congress had made no declaration of war (thus no crisis existed), and had not even recognized the existence of the conflict until July 13, 1861, while Lincoln had been violating the Constitution with what appeared to be great abandon prior to that time. A specific challenge went to the Supreme Court in 1862, during the war, and the Court concluded unambiguously *(Prize Cases* 2 Black 635, at 670):

> Whether the President in fulfilling his duties as Commander in Chief, in suppressing an insurrection, has met with such armed resistance, and a civil war of such alarming proportions as will compel him to accord to them the character of belligerents, is a question to be decided *by him,* and this Court must be governed by the decisions and acts of the political department of the Government to which this power was entrusted . . . . He must determine what degree of force the crisis demands.

The principle was thus established on constitutional grounds that, regardless of Congressional inaction, it is the President alone who determines whether a crisis exists and how much force is needed to suppress it. This remained the position of the Court throughout the crisis.

We now arrive at *Ex parte* Milligan. It is 1866. Lincoln has been assassinated. The war is over. Speaking for the majority, Justice David Davis pronounces the words cited by Senator Ervin: "No doctrine involving more pernicious consequences was ever invented by the wit of man than that any of its [the Constitution's] provisions can be suspended during any of the great exigencies of Government."

In the light of the background we have reviewed, Prof. Edward S. Corwin (widely acknowledged as one of the foremost experts on the Presidency) was moved to comment that the Milligan opinion was "an evident piece of arrant hypocrisy." *(The President: Office and Powers,* 2nd rev. ed., p. 163)

The principle of Abraham Lincoln that the nation's highest law is its own self-preservation has continued to exert a forceful influence in American history down to our day. Half a century after Lincoln the United States was beset by another internal crisis, of much less magnitude, but nonetheless quite real. This time it was the Sorelian revolutionary syndicalists who were disturbing the peace of American civil society. Again, a case challenging the prerogative of government — exercised this time by a state governor — to suspend fundamental constitutional guarantees reached the Supreme Court: *Moyer v. Peabody* 212 U.S. 78 (1909). The great liberal jurist, Oliver Wendall Holmes, delivered the majority opinion. And its grounds were readily intelligible even to ultra-liberal columnist Max Lerner who wrote of it in *The Mind and Faith of Justice Holmes: His Speeches, Essays, Letters, and Judicial Opinions* (Modern Library, pp. 269-70):

> Holmes's opinion is one of the leading constitutional cases on the relation of the executive power to martial rule . . . . There are three basic steps in his reasoning: as a general proposition, the executive process may be substituted for the judicial in a time of public danger; the Governor had the power, within his executive discretion, to declare a state of insurrection, call out the troops and order them to kill — and, since the larger power includes the lesser, he had the power to detain Moyer; although the detention proved to be "without sufficient reason," it was "in good faith." The implication is that, in the context of the necessities of the situation, good faith is all that the Court can require of the executive without crippling his power and therefore the survival of the state.

Holmes, Lerner concludes, was "fearful of any sentimentalism about liberty which would make effective government impossible in an emergency, 'Every society,' he was fond of saying, 'is founded upon the deaths of men.' If as a result of the era of world troubles, the United States ever finds itself again as a constitutional government on the verge of a civil conflict, Holmes's opinion will not only be invoked in putting down local insurrection, but by analogy the same reasoning will be transferred to Presidential Power."

The problem of Watergate is that it has almost hopelessly confused the entire issue — the prerogative power of the President as Commander in Chief and Chief Executive to preserve the sovereignty of the American nation. We have first a John Erlichman who *appeals* to the principle, but not so much — we suspect — in the interest of national security as in the interest of Richard Nixon's re-election. That appeal then evokes a torrent of abuse, rhetoric, misinformation, and spurious reasoning by the Ervins and Talmadges and the *New York Times.* And then we have Richard Nixon, who publicly agrees with Ervin and the *Times* and rejects the principle of Lincoln. Yet, we are led to wonder whether Mr. Nixon would not indeed be willing to use the *means* of Lincoln, the violation of the Constitution — at the whispered counsel of Kissinger — for an end quite alien to Lincoln, the surrender of American sovereignty.

Must the American patriot really be constrained to choose between the secret Kissinger-Nixon *real-politik* in the interest of destroying the nation, and the Dantean vision of a Sam Ervin standing amidst the flames of the funeral pyre that was once the American nation.

Connally vs. The Times

In its news columns of Sept. 12, 1973, the *New York Times* reported that John Connally said "the President might be justified in ignoring a Supreme Court decision to release the tapes. 'We're leading ourselves into believing the Supreme Court is the ultimate arbiter of all disputes,' he said, 'and I don't believe it. I think there are times when the President of the United States would be right in not obeying a decision of the Supreme Court.'"

In its editorial columns of the same issue an anonymous editorial writer for the *Times* responded to Mr. Connally with a typical *ex cathedra* pontification under the heading "Connally's Bad Advice":

This interpretation of constitutional government, which Mr. Connally appears to have discovered on the way to his conversion to "law and order" Republicanism, raises the question whether any force other than raw power would be left as the ultimate arbiter of controversial national issues. Even conceding that Mr. Connally for the moment appears to reserve for the President alone the right to ignore the Supreme Court, this redefinition of Presidential power strikes at the heart of democratic government as practiced in the United States for nearly 200 years . . . . What would be left of the principle of checks and balances? . . . Would President Truman have been justified in ignoring the Court's ruling on seizure of the steel mills? . . . Resort to impeachment would inevitably come to be thought of as a far less awesome step than has been the case in the past.

If the American people were to adopt the view that the President has the right to ignore the Supreme Court, then the Presidency will have been placed above the law. This would be the beginning of totalitarian rule.

Teddy Kennedy, ever ready to make political capital by jumping on any bandwagon (whether that of George Wallace or of the *Times*) within hours took the floor of the Senate to deliver an oration in which he states the same position — almost verbatim — as that of the *Times* editorial writer. Kennedy declared that if Nixon refused to abide by a Supreme Court decision on the tapes, the Senate [sic] would have no other recourse but to impeach him. Revealing his abysmal ignorance of the American political tradition, Kennedy cited as precedents to justify his position the examples of Jefferson, Jackson, F. D. Roosevelt, and Truman among others.

Thomas Jefferson, however, who is commonly regarded as an "apostle of liberal democracy," evidently was in complete disagreement with the *Times* editorial writer and Teddy Kennedy. On Connally's position, so far from seeing it as "striking at the heart of democratic government as practiced in the United States," Jefferson felt that only through that position could democratic government be preserved.

In 1819, Jefferson wrote:

> My construction of the Constitution is . . . . That each department is truly independent of the others, and has an equal right to decide for itself what is the meaning of the Constitution in the cases submitted to its action; and especially where it is to act ultimately and without appeal. . . . Each of the three departments has equally the right to decide for itself what is its duty under the Constitution, without any regard to what the others may have decided for themselves under a similar question.

As Alpheus T. Mason (one of our most prominent constitutional experts) has observed, Jefferson "could find nothing in the Constitution or in the theory of republican government giving to the Supreme Court an exclusive judgment in regard to the constitutionality of legislation. Each branch should pass on the validity of acts pertaining to matters within its jurisdiction." Is Jefferson thus to be considered an advocate of totalitarianism?

Under the administration of Andrew Jackson, the Supreme Court's Chief Justice John Marshall handed down a rigorous decision in *Worcester v. Georgia* (1832). President Jackson's reaction was: "John Marshall has made his decision, now let him enforce it." The decision was not enforced. Was Jackson, too, a wicked totalitarian?

In July 1963, Rexford G. Tugwell (former F.D.R. "braintruster" and currently a Senior Fellow at the Center for the Study of Democratic Institutions) addressed an audience at Harkness Theater in Columbia University. As the Columbia University newspaper reported,

> Tugwell decried "law-making" by the Court. Crucial issues came up, he said, on which the Court must not be allowed to block the President's use of his own conscience or Congress's legislative prerogatives. Referring to the Court's overruling of President Truman's order to take over the steel mills in 1952, Dr. Tugwell stated that

Truman could have done "an incalculable service" by defying the Court as Jackson once did (and as Chief Justice Vinson, in his dissent, felt that Truman might justifiably have done).

Were Tugwell and Chief Justice Vinson totalitarians? Or finally, was the former national director of the American Civil Liberties Union, Morris L. Ernst, a totalitarian when he wrote a book in the 1930s entitled *The Ultimate Power* in which he urged Presidential defiance of Court decisions?

Tragically for us today, Henry Kissinger has turned the meaning of "national security" inside out (see his "Definition of National Security Policy" in *Problems of National Strategy*, New York, 1965, p. 8, where he says explicitly that our society — our national union — need not survive to be "secure" in his sense). For that reason, when Mr. Nixon or Mr. Ehrlichman or Mr. Haldeman speak of "national security interests" we cannot assume that they mean what Washington, Jefferson, Jackson, Lincoln, or Lyndon Johnson understood the term to mean. Yet, if Mr. Nixon could honestly say that "genuine national security" interests would be betrayed by disclosure of his White House tapes, it would be, in the words of Jefferson, "absurdly sacrificing the end to the means" to scrupulously adhere to the Constitution, Congressional legislation, or a Supreme Court decision when it would jeopardize the national security of the United States as a sovereign nation.

There is abundant evidence in the American political tradition, from political leaders and scholars alike, that the Supreme Court is not to be considered the ultimate power in deciding what the Constitution means. However, even if we should accept the presumption that it is, there is no legitimate or logical ground for accepting the Ervin position that the Constitution must be preserved at all costs, as opposed to the Jefferson-Lincoln position that the nation must be preserved at all costs.

Despite the tragic inadequacies of Mr. Nixon, who

is, as Henry Paolucci aptly phrases it, a crippled, captive of anti-nationalist ideologues, the governmental principle at issue in this *Times*-Ervin-Connally dispute over presidential prerogatives remains this: Should only our alienated Ellsbergs and other "brilliant" analysts in Rand and Brookings have the prerogative power to decide what will affect and what will not affect national security and then be lionized for it by the liberal media? Is that where final authority for the governance of Americans shall reside hereafter? In that vast bundle of duplicities now known as the "Pentagon Papers" affair, the *New York Times* people claimed — indeed demanded — for themselves what they are now denying the President of the United States: the right to determine, after a careful scrutiny of secret documents, whether or not publication of them would adversely affect national security.

We owe it to the office of the President, if not to its present occupant, to defend the prerogatives of that office. The President is elected; he can be held accountable for his behavior. The publishers and editors of the *Times* are not elected; the people have no way of holding them accountable or responsible for the political power they wield. They arrogantly and self-righteously assume the power to judge what is and what is not a matter of national security. If we let them get away with that usurpation, we prove ourselves unworthy of our national heritage of free government. Our nation's safety is its highest law, and the prerogative powers to save it — as Lincoln saved it in the Civil War — are vested in its Presidency.

5. PROMETHEUS UNBOUND

If the major nations of the world, led by the United States and the Soviet Union, were to agree to give up their strategic weapons arsenals, and put an end to their organized capacities to produce replacement arms, would that mark the end of the "age of nuclear terror" that began in the closing months of World War II?

Back in the spring of 1978. at the time of the murder of Italy's former President Aldo Moro by terrorists of the Italian Red Brigades, James Reston of the *New York Times* morosely contemplated the problem of technological terrorism and concluded that the Moro killing was a "startling reminder of the fragility of all civilized nations." The trouble with civilized nations, he lamented, is that they persist in "worrying these days about classic wars of invasion across national borders, and they debate endlessly over cruise missiles, backfire bombers, and neutron artillery shells that can kill fleets of tanks." Yet there are obviously other kinds of warfare to worry about in our time, particularly the kinds involving technological terror, which "desperate minorities" are now increasingly capable of unleashing. In Reston's words:

> Any terrorist group, no matter how small, that knows what manholes to go down to get at the electrical guts of switches of any major city, can terrorize the life of that city. And as we move into the age of nuclear electric power, as we are bound to do as our petroleum supplies run out, the problem of sabotage is likely to become more serious. [If terrorists] can control a nuclear energy plant, or even a railroad train carrying nuclear wastes, they can hold whole cities and countries for ransom . . . . This is not a crazy speculation; it is a practical possibility

every country dealing with terrorists is now having to face.

Like most of his colleagues at the *Times,* James Reston is not much given to speculating about the means available to governments of civilized countries for coping with modern terrorism. And when he occasionally ventures a glance in that direction we are apt to see him shrinking back in disgust at the mere prospect of our American security agencies actually doing what they would plainly have to do to meet the challenge of violent minorities equipped to terrorize civilized majorities.

On this point, let us not delude ourselves. The political uses of nuclear blackmail and the opportunities for it are very great. A usual response when such a charge is made is that the "destructive power of weapons in the hands of the state" is incomparably greater than anything the terrorists could make use of. The point, however, is this: terrorists are likely to use nuclear and other weapons of mass destruction against the state, but a government — and particularly a news-media-dominated popular government like ours — is less likely to use such weapons against terrorists. Who then has more power?

What in fact has our Government's response to this threat been? The answer, without mincing words, is that all Federal agencies concerned have been grossly derelict in their responsibilities; and, worse, some have at times engaged in a massive cover up. Unlike the Watergate cover up, the exposure of which served only to open up money-making careers for most of the people involved in its trivialities, this one can materially affect the lives of all Americans and millions upon millions of others in the non-Communist industrial nations.

National Review's "Prometheus Bound"

But if news-media people of the caliber of James Reston shrink in horror from the spectacle of what may *yet* prove to be the necessities of crisis government, and if the

major agencies of our establishment-dominated government engage in what amounts to a cover up, what about the
security-conscious publicists of the "new guard" on the
political and ideological right? What do the editors of
William F. Buckley's *National Review,* for instance, think of
the risks we face of terrorists gaining control of massive
quantities of poisonous nuclear wastes, or stealing sufficient amounts of uranium/plutonium to make nuclear
devices, or even seizing an entire nuclear energy plant?

One might assume, without specific inquiry, that all
of our nation's conservative opinion-makers would be of
one mind in assessing the gravity of our situation in this
sphere. Has our government the moral will or even the
"security intelligence" to safeguard our nuclear materials
against terrorists or the "hit teams" of powerful "potential
adversaries"? According to the hardliners at *National Review* and most other conservative publications, our security
intelligence is now virtually non-existent. Quite typical are
these words of M. Stanton Evans in the July 6, 1979 issue of
National Review:

> The crippling of U.S. intelligence capabilities has been a
> major goal of liberal forces in recent years — a goal that
> they have triumphantly attained. Thanks to a steady
> drumfire of criticism in the press, congressional ex-
> poses, denunciations by defecting agents, and agitprop
> from Communist sources, the Central Intelligence
> Agency, along with the FBI and other security agencies,
> has been effectively throttled. [All of this] has put the
> intelligence community in shock, and made it afraid to
> lift a finger in its own behalf. Throughout this orgy of
> recrimination, the liberal media and liberal forces in the
> Congress have served as cheering sections for the anti-
> intelligence crusade. And now . . . the Senate is contem-
> plating further restrictive measures that . . . would bring
> effective U.S. intelligence efforts to a grinding halt.

If that indictment is true, would it be reasonable for
security-conscious conservatives to feel confident that our

Government is capable of securing our nuclear installations against "penetration" by terrorists or, worse, the highly-trained hit-squads of needy friends or determined foes? According to *National Review's* special issue on nuclear power (February 2, 1979) — titled "Prometheus Bound" and characterized by its editors as "unique in the history of the magazine" — the answer to our question ought to be, apparently, a resounding Yes! Its very title suggests assurances that we have little to fear; the ancient Promethean gift of fire, which man has ingeniously developed into an explosive power capable of reducing our planet to a smoldering ash (*solvet saeclum in favilla*) as the old hymn had prophesied, is not out of control but, rather, safely bound to a cliff. That, at any rate, is the explicit argument of Bernard L. Cohen's featured article, which "demonstrates that nuclear power is both safe and necessary," as also of the companion piece by B. Bruce-Briggs titled "Terror and Anxiety" — which is an extended review of the books *Nuclear Theft: Risks and Safe Guards* (1974), by Mason Willrich and Theodore B. Taylor, and *The Curve of Binding Energy* (also 1974), by John McPhee. In addition to Cohen and Bruce-Briggs, the editors of the "Prometheus Bound" issue of *National Review* had enlisted the intelligence of fifteen other confident "experts" to deal with related aspects of its theme in ways that support the optimism of its title.

An introductory note explained that the idea of a special issue on nuclear power had grown out of the response to an earlier article by Professor Cohen, "The Case for the Breeder Reactor" in the September 16, 1977 issue of *National Review.* In the earlier article, Cohen's avowed purpose had been to confront and dismiss any problem of nuclear terrorism. Since the terrorist group's capacity to engage in nuclear terrorism is obviously dependent upon technological expertise and obtaining weapons-grade materials, Cohen focused his inquiry first of all on those two aspects of the subject.

By way of background, one should note at this point that for years Government spokesmen — excepting only some in the highly-disciplined GAO (General Accounting Office) — had consistently denied that the technical knowledge needed to engage in nuclear terrorism was readily available or that it could be mastered by potential terrorists. More recently they have had to acknowledge that the technology is available and that fabrication of a bomb is not especially difficult; but most of them have continued to insist that the necessary materials are inaccessible because of "increasingly stringent security precautions." Thus, if the latter claim were *not* true — if the necessary materials *were* accessible — then obviously our security would hereafter depend solely upon the humanitarian impulses of the terrorist, the psychotic, and the criminal.

In both the 1977 and the 1979 articles Professor Cohen stresses: (1) that the needed uranium/plutonium has become increasingly inaccessible to terrorists — "in thirty years, there has never even been a theft attempt, and safeguarding techniques are improving rapidly"; (2) that to design a nuclear bomb is far more difficult than procuring the materials — since it "requires reasonable expertise in nuclear reactor physics, hydrodynamics, computation techniques, chemistry, electronics, and high-explosive technology, plus some familiarity with health physics"; (3) that to proceed from designing to actually fabricating a device is even more difficult — since it "would require thousands of dollars' worth of equipment and would take many weeks or months of concerted effort"; and (4) even if terrorists could get this far, it wouldn't be worth their while — since, with "all this effort and risk," the most that could be done would be to "kill the occupants of a large building," and there are "many easier ways to accomplish that end."

The Record on Nuclear Thefts

How much truth is there in Professor Cohen's reassuring assertions that the "possibility of stealing enough

plutonium to make a bomb is now very remote," and that
there is "no evidence that any significant amount of plutonium was ever diverted for illegal uses"?

We reserve for later our extended discussion of the
large quantities of highly enriched uranium which were
reported missing, and had apparently been "diverted"
from the small nuclear facility at Apollo, Pennsylvania.
Here we note only that, as if to mock Professor Cohen most
directly, during the very week when *National Review's*
"Prometheus Bound" issue was on the newstand, the AP,
the UPI, and the *New York Times* seemed to vie with one
another in reporting significant thefts of plutonium/ura-
nium in transit. AP reported that on February 1, 1979, a
worker at General Electric had broken into a 275-pound
container of uranium and had stolen 150 pounds as part of
an extortion scheme. On February 9, UPI reported that
Federal agents were holding two men in connection with
the seizure of 5,000 pounds of stolen uranium that was
apparently on its way to an unidentified buyer in El Paso,
and that, three months before, two 1000-pound barrels of
stolen uranium had had been seized in Albuquerque.

All the *New York Times* could report during the week
of February 2, 1979, was that a Nuclear Regulatory Commission inspector drove through the gate of an upstate
New York nuclear power plant without being challenged.
But just a month earlier (January 4, 1979), it had reported
an official acknowledgement from Washington that "a
consignment of nuclear fuel" destined for Roumania had
been "tampered with before the shipment left the United
States." The report specified that the

> seals placed on four canisters of highly enriched ura-
> nium . . . to deter possible efforts to remove the weapons-
> grade material had been broken . . . . The Federal
> officials were said to have replaced the broken seals and
> to have sent the canisters through to Roumania on Dec.
> 16 without checking whether any of the enriched ura-
> nium had been removed . . . . The incident had set off a

dispute in which the State Department aides are complaining about the apparent laxity of the Nuclear Regulatory Commission.

But what about the nuclear plants themselves? In his 1979 article Professor Cohen had assured readers of *National Review* that our plutonium stores are safe against terrorist theft because, in coming out of the heavily guarded storage areas, even "people with special clearance . . . have to pass through monitors which are capable of detecting very small amounts." Again as if to mock his assurances, in March 1979, several publications revealed that there was now in circulation a report published by the NRC itself, titled *The Barrier Penetration Database*, which gave precise instructions on how to break through sensors, doors, walls, ceilings, or any of 32 barriers that an intruder at a nuclear power plant might encounter.

NRC officials hastened to explain that circulation of the report was deemed necessary "to supply the NRC and nuclear power plant licensees with basic data" about what tools intruders would have to have and just how long it would actually take them to break in. Critics of the report contended that it obviously combined all the information any serious terrorists would need." All the nuclear plants are concerned about this," said Leon Russell, chief engineer at the Calvert Cliffs Nuclear Plant in Baltimore, since "making such information public almost dares certain people to try to break into a power plant." Had it been a mistake to publish the report? No, Said Dr. Anthony Fainberg of the Brookhaven National laboratory, one of its co-authors. "This gives the crazy person a little bit more data than he would otherwise have," Dr. Fainberg acknowledged: "But the overwhelming benefits of allowing the free flow of information more than offset the very miniscule possible risk that is involved in this case." Obviously for Fainberg, as for Dr. Cohen, Prometheus remains securely bound, since only a "crazy person" would want to break in and steal his fire power.

Difficulties of Bomb-Designing and Bomb-Making

Where are the terrorists who, even if they managed to steal enough plutonium or uranium, would know how to design and actually build a nuclear device? Haven't there been TV and newspaper reports in depth about how first a student from MIT, then one from Princeton, then a third from Harvard, had succeeded in designing "workable" bombs even though they lacked serious technical training and could consult only unclassified books? In his 1979 article, Professor Cohen attacks and contemptuously dismisses the very idea of student designed bombs. Moreover, he adds with confidence, "nobody who's ever worked on our atomic bomb project" would presume to say whether "some particular design would or would not work" because he "would be divulging very secret information" in violation of the law.

But Professor Cohen is on all counts wrong on this subject, and he ought to have known it. Less than a year earlier, the Senate Sub-committee on Nuclear Proliferation, headed by former astronaut John Glenn, had heard testimony from "a 22-year-old former Harvard student with only one year of college-level physics" about how he had "designed a series of nuclear weapons . . . in the last five months from material that was available to the public and without the help of any government, corporation, or person." According to the *Times* report of March 22, 1978, two scientists with many years of experience in designing atomic weapons had done precisely what Professor Cohen had said such experts would not do: they had told the Sub-committee that the young student had done an unusually proficient job, that his design was indeed workable. One of the expert witnesses was Dr. Theodore B. Taylor who, from 1949 to 1956, had been a member of the team designing nuclear weapons at the Los Alamos laboratory in New Mexico — an expert for whom Dr. Cohen professes high respect. The young student's manuscript on the subject, Taylor testified, "is the most extensive and detailed expo-

sition that I have seen outside of classified literature."
According to Senator Glenn, the central fact borne
out by the expert testimony at his Sub-committee hearings
was that initial lack of knowledge of nuclear weapons was
no longer a barrier to their manufacture. "In other words,"
he said, "if the mechanical equipment of the bomb is
available, the only lacking ingredient for a truly workable
bomb is uranium enriched to weapons grade or plutonium."

The Uses of Nuclear Terrorism

But what sort of "expert" is Professor Cohen? Certainly he is not an "expert" bomb-maker, like Dr. Taylor. As
he quite candidly acknowledges in his 1979 article: "I
personally would not know how to build a nuclear bomb,
as I have never been involved in that sort of work." What
he presumes to be an expert on is evidently the "mentality"
of terrorists and the "uses" to which nuclear terrorism is
now limited. And in that sort of expertise he is joined by B.
Bruce-Briggs, author of the companion-piece on "Terror
and Anxiety" published in the same "Prometheus Bound"
issue of *National Review*.

We noted earlier Cohen's basic contention that
terrorists wouldn't build a nuclear bomb even if they could
because all they could do with it was kill the inhabitants of
a large building, which they could as easily do, in his words,
by "releasing a poisonous gas" in its ventilation system.
Terrorists know, says Cohen, that, with far less trouble
than it takes to make a bomb, they could kill at least as
many people by using "conventional explosives or incendi-
aries in large crowds, as at sports stadiums"; and that they
could obviously kill many more by "blowing open a large
dam," or by poisoning "a city's water or food supplies."
Any of these measures, Cohen concludes, "would be sim-
pler, safer, cheaper, and faster than stealing plutonium
and making a bomb." Ergo: there can be no risk at all that,
despite the collapse of our security agencies, terrorists will

not so much as want to unbind our Prometheus, much less succeed in doing so.

Bruce-Briggs does, however, admit that "a gang of serious terrorists or criminals could knock over a nuclear power or fuel-processing facility and obtain fissionable materials." But then he repeats Cohen's arguments that (1) most terrorists wouldn't know what to do with such materials, and that (2) if one of them could conceivably design a bomb, why would he want to "fool with atomic devices, which are easily detected through radiation, when he could kill or threaten multitudes with means more readily at hand — such as, to take the most obvious method, poisoning water supplies?"

The answer to Bruce-Briggs and Cohen lies in the rather obvious fact that the true purpose of terrorism is not to kill people but, quite simply, to terrorize. True terrorism is political theater, and its essential imperative is this: You kill some people in order to terrorize those you don't kill. Conventional explosives, however destructive, have ceased to terrorize our generation in any theatrical sense. Putting poison in the ventilation system of a large building can be passed off by a government as some as yet unidentified new virus. And the other chemical and biological options suggested by Bruce-Briggs and Cohen can be similarly passed off. But no nuclear explosion, however small, can be explained away in that fashion. Dr. Cohen nowhere takes up the question of a credible nuclear-terrorist threat. In its place he prefers to insist, as we have seen, that it is one thing to design a bomb and quite another to fabricate one — since everything is so hard to get and costly to do. Yet thousands of pounds of plutonium and uranium are in fact currently missing. If the Government at some point receives a threat with sophisticated bomb designs, what then does it do? Does it cave in to the blackmail? Or does it ignore the threat and risk a major disaster? Perhaps Dr. Cohen can tell the Government.

Or alternately, he might advise us all to join Bruce-

Briggs in the comforting assumption that "terrorists are all basically incompetent." The truth on this subject, Bruce-Briggs alleges, "is summed up in an Israeli explanation of the miserable performance of the Arab terrorists: 'The Palestinians have good jobs in Kuwait: P.L.O. is the dregs.' .... terrorism is for losers." But surely Bruce-Briggs knows that Israel, at any rate, has in the past produced terrorists who were not losers, not incompetents. And so have many other nations. He comes close to admitting this where he acknowledges that, "as Lewis A. Dunn of the Hudson Institute has emphasized, the worst threat to nuclear materials is from commando units or intelligence agents of foreign governments." He here adds a parenthetical remark — "(A state friendly to the U.S. is widely believed to have been hijacking already.)" — but graciously refrains from identifying the friendly and thoroughly competent hijacker. Needless to say — and here we cross over into the sphere of the second focus of our study — the state in question is plainly Israel, whose government has a much more realistic sense of the dangers and uses of nuclear terrorism than our own has ever had.

6. THE APOLLO DIVERSION

What had in fact come to be widely believed at the time Bruce-Briggs wrote his article for the "Prometheus Bound" issue of *National Review* was that the State of Israel — certainly friendly to the United States at the time — had begun hijacking uranium in transit on the high seas sometime in the late 1960s. Before that, Israel had apparently been able to get uranium out of the U.S. simply by smuggling; but when the smuggling was detected and had to stop, "hijacking and clandestine purchases," soon enough proved themselves to be viable alternatives.

As it has actually unravelled itself in the American news-media, the story of Israel's extra-legal efforts to acquire materials for its physical and psychological security against the potential of Arab technological terrorism begins with a UPI report of May 9, 1977. B. Bruce-Briggs may have seen it, for it had to do with uranium hijacking at sea. Some days earlier, the London *Observer* had reported the arrest in Norway of a member of an Israeli "hit team" which had allegedly killed eleven Arab terrorists in Europe. The man had been charged with murder; and to escape the penalty for that crime he had evidently plea-bargained with the Norwegian authorities, confessing instead to the lesser crime of having hijacked uranium into Israel many years before.

According to Norwegian authorities, the Israeli hit-team sharpshooter very obviously knew the "whole story" of what had happened in 1968 to a German freighter which had been carrying "enough uranium to build 42 nuclear bombs." In the UPI account we read: "The disappearance of the uranium cargo in 1968 was disclosed April 30, [1977] in a speech by Paul Leventhal, a former counsel to a United

States Senate Committee at a nuclear conference in Salzburg, Australia." Israeli agents had been negotiating to purchase the vessel in question and therefore had a purchaser's access to it. Quite inexplicably it disappeared from sight for a while; and then, as Paul Leventhal explained in Salzburg, it turned up again, in a few weeks, "with a new name, a new registry, a new crew but no uranium." Less than a year later, that same Paul Levanthal would publish an entire book on the subject, characterizing the "case of the phantom uranium ship" as "one of the world's best kept secrets," confirmed, as he put it, only to a "select group of nuclear officials, diplomats, and intelligence agents." But before commenting on that book, we have to trace at least in outline the gradual build-up of evidence of thefts or diversions of nuclear materials not in transit, as in the case of the phantom uranium freighter, but directly from American plants.

Theft for a Good Cause?

On July 4, 1977 — just two months after the phantom uranium-ship hijack disclosures of the London *Observer* and UPI — David Burnham of the *New York Times* began what proved to be an annual series of articles (at least three have appeared each year since the first) on official Government reports concerning "several curious developments" at a small nuclear facility in Apollo, Pennsylvania. Mr. Burnham disclosed, first of all, that the Apollo facility had been cited by Government inspectors for having repeatedly violated basic "safety and security regulations," but that it had nevertheless continued to receive Government contracts worth millions of dollars. In Burnham's words;

> The most serious of the hundreds of violations cited over the last 20 years was a 1965 finding that the facility could not account for 381.6 pounds of highly enriched uranium, enough to serve as raw material for at least 10 nuclear bombs. Government officials have contended

that the material was lost in complicated manufacturing processes and was not stolen.

The trouble with that explanation, Burnham went on, is that rigorous General Accounting Office (GAO) inspectors severely discount it and even the Nuclear Regulatory Commission (NRC) doesn't believe it. In June 1975, the NRC had in fact issued a 90-page summary of the chronic enforcement problems at the Apollo facility; and in it we read at one point: "The loss of highly enriched uranium prompted the AEC [Atomic Energy Commission] to question 400 persons and refer the case to the FBI. For reasons that are not clear, the FBI decided not to investigate." Upon reviewing the summary, the NRC regional director said: "This obviously was our worst performer"; but the founder and first president of the Apollo facility, Zalman A. Shapiro, could be brought to say only: "We operated within the rules and regulations."

Burnham began his chronicle of violations at the Apollo facility with an inspector's report of 1960 which concluded that "the company did not have adequate control over the nuclear material in its possession," and which was followed, in 1964, by "another finding that internal control procedures were inadequate and that the uranium reports being submitted were not complete and not factual." On March 23, 1965, the Apollo directors were told that the Government would bill them $2.8 million for 657 pounds of uranium that "could not be found." Burnham dutifully notes here that both the old Atomic Energy Commission (AEC) and the Nuclear Regulatory Commission (NRC) that succeeded it "have repeatedly asserted that there was no evidence that the highly enriched uranium had been obtained by any unauthorized person or nation." But, not less dutifully, he then reviews the General Accounting Office's far less reassuring appraisal of the situation:

> The GAO said it could not come to a definite conclusion about what had happened to the uranium. The condition

of the company records, the summary reported, did not permit the GAO auditors to make a conclusive determination as to the time or the manner in which the losses occurred. An FBI spokesman, in response to an inquiry, declined to comment on why the bureau had chosen not to investigate. Three separate officials familiar with the case, however, reported that the FBI did investigate whether a senior official of the Apollo facility was an agent for a foreign country. The investigation, one official said, found no evidence that he was.

Which senior official? Which foreign country? For specific answers in this regard we have to wait for David Burnham's article of August 4, 1977 — exactly one month after the first. The Government had that very day, Burnham noted, for the very first time published reports with concrete figures on the overall dimension of the problem of nuclear materials currently categorized as MUF (missing or unaccounted for). Unofficial estimates were much higher; but the government report was that 8,000 pounds of highly enriched uranium and plutonium were missing. Again it was specified that the facility at Apollo, Pennsylvania, appeared to be a principal offender, with respect to safeguards. Clarifying his remark of a month earlier, Burnham notes that the unaccounted for "losses" at that facility had led to an investigation by the FBI, and a separate investigation by the CIA, to determine whether one of the facility's top executives was an agent of a foreign nation.

Though the AEC had "concluded that there was no evidence of theft," Burnham wrote, "several intelligence officials have said there was widespread speculation that the uranium may have been stolen by agents of another country, specifically Israel." In his follow-up article of August 8, 1977, the *Times'* specialist on nuclear-theft news added a detail that, according to a House of Representatives investigator, U.S. intelligence officials had "strong suspicions that highly enriched uranium, the type that could be used in bombs, was stolen from a Pennsylvania

nuclear facility more than a decade ago." Why had the FBI
declined to investigate the "strong suspicions" and "widespread speculation" of possible Israeli theft of the materials reported missing at Apollo? On October 18, 1977, the
Associated Press reported on evidence that, in 1966, president Johnson very explicitly "told Richard Helms, then
director of CIA, not to pursue an investigation of why 400
pounds of bomb-grade uranium was missing from a Pennsylvania fuel plant," even though Helms had said the CIA
was convinced uranium had been diverted to Israel. (When
contacted on October 17, Helms had dutifully refused to
discuss the matter; so had the Carter White House a week
later — though Press Secretary Jody Powell subsequently
told reporters that "four years of continual investigation by
the AEC, the FBI, and the GAO all failed to reveal that such
diversions did occur." Responding to calls from the *Times,*
the Israeli Embassy in Washington reportedly said: "The
wording of Mr. Powell's statement today seemed to indicate that as far as President Carter was concerned the
investigations into possible theft from the United States
nuclear facilities were now a closed matter and would not
be pursued." The account in the *Times* cautiously explained: "It may be that the Carter Administration, which
has had uneasy relations with Israel and its supporters . . .
does not wish to open another possible source of friction."

A month later, both the *Washington Post* and the
New York Times discussed at length the substance of an
article by Howard Kahn and Barbara Newman that had
originally appeared in *Rolling Stone* magazine. It alleged
that, in the late 1960s, Israel had purchased uranium from
West Germany and France under the cover of staged
hijackings. Two real hijackings of uranium occurred in
1968, apparently, but then two more were staged with the
cooperation of West Germany, which received "full pay-
ment," though clandestinely, in cash and scientific information. Cohen and Newman commented that Israel had
undertaken the hijackings and clandestine purchases only

after it was forced to halt a 10-year smuggling operation, which had netted it from 200 to 400 pounds of bomb-grade uranium from the processing plant at Apollo, Pennsylvania. "The stolen material," Kohn and Newman concluded, was of course "used to give Israel a last resort military alternative in the Mideast."

Both the *Post* and the *Times* accounts denied that the Kohn-Newman article had solid evidence to support it. And so did the Israeli Embassy and Defense Secretary Harold Brown, when questioned on November 27, 1977. But by then the *Times* already had in its possession "two classified documents written in 1976" that linked the uranium missing from the Apollo plant with Israel. And, according to David Burnham, other documents, obtained under the Freedom of Information Act, showed that many officials in the old AEC were deeply concerned about the way the president of the Apollo facility, Dr. Shapiro, ran his plant, which employed several alien technicians and often admitted alien visitors. According to Burnham, a secret summary of the case, apparently prepared for President Ford in 1975, contained the following:

> Harold Ungar, a Washington lawyer now representing Dr. Shapiro, said his client's position is "very simple: he never diverted a single microgram of nuclear material to Israel or anyone else and does not believe that anyone else did so at the plant." Mr. Ungar also said: "If they're pursuing Dr. Shapiro because he is Jewish and a Zionist, for which he offers no apologies, it's a hell of a basis for an investigation."

The documents used by Burnham were later evaluated by the *Christian Science Monitor* {November 15, 1977) and explored in greater depth. What "the released documents and interviews with several people who ought to know much of what there is to know . . . reveal," we read in that issue of *CSM* "is that the plant in Pennsylvania failed for a considerable period in the 1960s to maintain adequate safeguards and bookkeeping and that the plant's president had, according to a 1968 FBI report, 'very close ties with Israel.'. . . There was a feeling among some congressional sources that people in high places covered something up. But . . .'the trail is cold,' said one congressional specialist who had studied the matter."

According to one document, the *Christian Science Monitor* account continued, "Zalman H. Shapiro, the company's owner and president, contended that at one point most of the material unaccounted for was probably to be found in burial pits at the plant. After many meetings and discussions, Mr. Shapiro was forced to have the buried materials dug up, but the results showed clearly that not more than about 5% of the more than 100 pounds unaccounted for at that stage could be recovered. The documents showed that Mr, Shapiro had several commercial contracts with Israel. His company was a sales agent for the Government of Israel through its ministry of defense. An FBI report said Mr. Shapiro was part of a 'highly organized effort on the part of Israel in the United States to obtain substantial technical and financial assistance.'"

The Apollo Haven: A Long Way from Watergate

In the early months of 1978 — which is to say, a whole year before *National Review* published Bernard L. Cohen's emphatic assurances about "stringent safeguards" against theft at our nuclear plants — discussion of the Apollo diversions became much more open.

Had Dr .Cohen read only the David Burnham *Times* articles of January 26, February 28, and March 2, 1978, he would have known (1) that the CIA had "concluded as early as 1974 — two years earlier than previously indicated — that Israel had already produced atomic weapons, partly with uranium it had obtained by clandestine means"; (2) that Lee v. Gossick, Executive Director of the Nuclear Regulatory Commission, who had originally told a congressional committee that there was no evidence of theft at the Apollo plant, had subsequently retracted that statement; and (3) that a CIA document had been inadvertently released disclosing that the CIA had informed President Johnson in 1968 that Israel had nuclear bombs made largely with the use of clandestinely procured materials, whereupon President Johnson had instructed the agency "not to tell anyone else, not even Dean Rusk and Robert McNamara."

Most interesting is Burnham's account of Lee V. Gossick's initial appearance before the House Subcommittee on Energy and Environment which was looking into reports of thefts at nuclear plants. "At one point in his testimony," Burnham wrote, the Executive Director of the NRC "said that every possible case of diversion had been investigated and we have no evidence that a significant amount of special nuclear material was stolen. A few minutes later, when specifically asked about Apollo, Mr. Gossick said he was not familiar with the alleged circumstances about that." Two days later, Gossick in fact "acknowledged that his first statement was not 'in full compliance' with the obligation to keep Congress 'fully and currently informed.'" But by then the House Subcommittee was hearing testimony from Dr .Victor Gilinsky, one of the four sitting Commissioners of the Nuclear Agency, who acknowledged that, with respect to the Apollo facility, "the Commission's obligation to keep Congress informed had not been 'discharged in the manner I would want to do it in the future,' and that Mr. Gossick's original statement 'really does not pass muster.'"

The revelation about President Johnson's order to the CIA, through its Director, Richard Helms, not to tell his Secretaries of State and Defense about the "Apollo-Israel diversions" was part of a four-page interview with Carl Duckett, the CIA's former Deputy Director for Science and Technology, inadvertently included in a "550-page report by the NRC concerning what the Commission knew or did not know about the possible theft of nuclear material that could be made into atomic bombs." Mr. Duckett had discussed the Apollo situation with heads of

the Nuclear Agency, and he recalls that, when details were
being laid out, one Commissioner had commented with
mock jocularity: "My God, I almost went to work with Zal
Shapiro. I came close to working for him." David Burnham
then adds: "Dr. Edward A. Mason, who was a Commissioner in 1976 and who is now a Vice President of the
Standard Oil Company . . . confirmed in a telephone
conversation today [March 2, 1978] that he had made
approximately the statement attributed to him and that he
was referring to Dr. Zalman Shapiro, the former President
of a nuclear facility in Apollo Pennsylvania."

On March 23, 1978, when there was no longer any
possibility of further blanket concealment of nuclear theft
— except perhaps from readers of Bernard L. Cohen's
articles in *National Review* — the Washington *Star* published
this summary:

> The AEC decided in 1966 to conceal a loss of nuclear
> materials from the public on the ground that premature
> disclosure "could lead to sensational and probably inac-
> curate press reports." According to a previously secret
> document made public today by the Senate Government
> Affairs Committee the issue was the unexplained loss of
> 202 pounds of highly enriched uranium from a plant in
> Apollo, Pennsylvania . . . . Howard C. Brown, then the
> Agency's General Manager, conceded that because the
> safeguard system then rested on a "presumption of
> honesty" it "might not reveal a deliberate and systematic
> attempt to divert nuclear material to a foreign govern-
> ment." AEC officials resolved their problems by develop-
> ing a "theory" that the company had lost the uranium by
> consistently underestimating its waste over a number of
> years."

By March, 1978, Paul Leventhal had published his
book about the "case of the phantom uranium ship" which
had vanished for a few days back in 1968. Leventhal called
his book *The Plumbat Affair* because the "220 tons of
uranium" that disappeared from the ship had been carried
in drums mislabelled "Plumbat." In an *Op-Ed* article for the

Times, Leventhal observed that "belated detection of a
diversion, as in the *Plumbat* case, offers no guarantee that
the diversion will be publicly announced and acted upon";
and as for the gravity of that particular diversion, he added:

> The use of this material in reactors of the type operating
> in Israel and India at the time could produce enough
> products of plutonium for as many as 40 atomic bombs
> over 20 years.

7. AN ACCUMULATION OF TROUBLE

We suggested earlier that the recent literature on the subject of nuclear terrorism (both in the category of professional studies and works by "experts" addressing a popular market) tends by and large to exploit the temporary excitements and then to play down the danger and even warn, finally, against "over-reaction". The same tendency or pattern is discernible in most government reports on the subject — the one notable exception being some of the major reports of the General Accounting Office (GAO).

The promising response of several government agencies to the surfacing of reports about diversions, hijackings, and clandestine purchases of nuclear materials early in 1979, and anticipating deeper congressional or news-media probes, many bureaucrats on all levels began making moves to cover themselves. Even so, as late as March 21, 1978, the cover-up on the Apollo situation was still very much in effect. On that date, David Burnham revealed in the *Times* that the GAO had accused the Attorney General and the Director of the CIA of illegally blocking the access of congressional investigators to secret intelligence files.

We should mention here, for purposes of background, that under an intentionally broad grant of authority from Congress, the GAO is legally entitled to have easy access to classified documents in the executive branch. All agencies are required to furnish any information and documents that GAO's investigators request — the only exemption, under the law, as Burnham noted, being information as to "specific funds requested by either the head of CIA or the Attorney General for an unforeseen emergency."

Specifically, what prompted Burnham's comments on the subject in late March 1979 was disclosure of the contents of a letter from the Comptroller General of the United States, Elmer B. Staats, to the chairman of the House Sub-committee on Energy and Power — Democratic Representative Dingell of Michigan — in which the Comptroller General charged that, in 1978 the GAO was refused permission to examine classified data about the uranium discovered missing from the Apollo plant fifteen years ago. When asked about the Comptroller General's charge, spokesmen for both the CIA and the Attorney General, Burnham noted, refused to comment. Mr. Staats had written to Representative Dingell, Burnham further noted, because Dingell had charged in a letter of December 27, 1978 that failure to allow a full congressional investigation of the uranium unaccounted for at the Apollo plant "raised basic questions about the performance of the FBI, the CIA, and other agencies in attempting to determine whether the material was stolen."

There is a piece of powerful irony here. The evidence is abundant that the FBI and CIA had done their duty and that high elective and appointive officials had engaged in a cover-up. Yet when Representative Dingell's charges were first disclosed, John Shattuck and Jerry J. Berman of the American Civil Liberties Union (ACLU), David Cohen of Common Cause, and Morton H. Halperin of the Center for National Security Studies used the disclosures rather cynically to attack the FBI and the CIA as being "still out of control."

The reality, we must not hesitate to say, is that Presidents Johnson, Nixon, Ford, and now Carter have connived in the Apollo diversions cover-up. And with this particular cover-up the media have been unusually compliant. In fact, the media and top-level political figures have cunningly contrived through various sleights-of-hand to obvert the entire situation. For what are at best partisan electoral concerns and at worst interests of conspiratorial collusion with operatives of foreign nations, responsibility has been shifted away from the high officials in ultimate control of the security agencies to the agencies themselves.

What Is to Be Done?

In a syndicated column released for publication on November 18, 1977, Gary Wills, a former editor and major contributor of *National Review,* had observed that the "story of Israel's hijackings and smugglings of enriched uranium raises troubling questions." Having seen the evidence then available about German phantom freighters and uranium diversions in Pennsylvania, Wills charged the American Government with what he said amounted to complicity in potential nuclear blackmail. "Our Government," he charged, was certainly "as complicitous as Germany's in creating another nuclear power. The commandos did not have to seize our uranium, because we were quietly slipping it to them."

But, why not slip uranium for atomic bombs to Israel? Don't we, doesn't the entire West, "owe it" to the Israelis — "as survivors of the holocaust" — to provide them with ultimate weapons of resistance in the Mideast? Gary Wills' answer, addressed to a leadership made up primarily of persons highly sympathetic to the national security needs of Israel, ran as, follows:

> Israel is currently our ally. But George Washington warned, in his Farewell Address, against presuming the nation will forever maintain the same relations of friendship and hostility. A different sort of regime, or an Israeli panic into irresponsible action, might possess a blackmail power over us if we help give them the bomb. The country can make demands of this sort: "Give us all the non-nuclear weapons we want, to use any way we want, or we will be forced to use the nuclear bomb you helped us get." Are we willing to support any Israeli action under that kind of blackmail? These questions become more acute when we remember that Israeli Prime Minis-

ter Menachem Begin may have his finger on the nuclear button. A man with heart trouble, recently hospitalized for exhaustion, with a terrorist background and maximal demands on territory — are we sure we would support any action he might take against the inhabitants of the West Bank?"

Those are fair questions — given the fact that the United States has never shown a comparable concern to "slip" materials for weapons of ultimate security to other "embattled allies," in Southeast Asia, Africa, or South America, for instance. And perhaps, had he still been on good terms with his old friends at *National Review,* Mr. Wills might conceivably have been called upon to raise questions of that kind for the "Prometheus Bound" issue of February, 1979 — to counterbalance some of Dr. Cohen's exaggerations in the opposite direction.

Dr. Cohen's arguments for breeder reactors and against worrying about safeguards at nuclear plants, as well as those of B. Bruce-Briggs, qualify as conservative or "right-wing" arguments only because they were published in *National Review* and purportedly take the side of "free-enterprise" — at Apollo, Pennsylvania, and elsewhere — against the "antinuclear lobbyists" of the left. But in substance they are arguments, we need to stress, that simply repeat the analysis of the uses of terrorism supplied by Lenin in *Partisan Warfare* and Trotsky in various works. Both of them had contended, long before they actually organized the terror of their Russian Revolution, that neither terrorism nor guerrilla warfare was sufficient to overthrow the capitalist state. As capitalism developed, they both reasoned, state power grew stronger and more concentrated. Terrorist instruments therefore could only be at best adjuncts to the mass convulsive uprising.

But in this Trotsky and Lenin were both wrong. They failed to take account — as George Sorel later explained in *Reflections on Violence* — of the unwillingness of bourgeois-liberal elites to use the power at their command.

They also failed to realize the significance of the enormous developments occurring in the technology of weapons.

Throughout history weaponry has undergone certain technological developments that have always been intimately related to whoever holds political power in a state. And that is because the ultimate source of political authority is coercive power. In the Homeric period of classical Greece, the virtuoso knights — the skilled noblemen — were the dominant force. To be a knight required a certain economic substance. One needed sufficient wealth for a horse and the long period of training it took to learn how to use the weapons. During the Middle Ages (with which we are imaginatively more familiar) that was also true, of Saracens as well as Christian crusaders.

But then came the great democratic invention of firearms. Firearms required little skill to use, and therefore tended to make each person equal to everyone else. To this day, among criminal subcultures and the military the firearm is still referred to as "an equalizer." That amounted to a new beginning. But soon more sophisticated firearms were developed, which in turn led to aristocratic-oligarchic political effects. Automatic weapons, artillery, and air power were usually beyond the scope of the average person. And then in 1945 came atomic weaponry. That seemed to mean that now the most powerful nations — which were alone capable of producing such weapons — would dominate the world, and permanently. Since then, however, we have had another great "democratic" advance in weapons technology. Atomic or nuclear weapons, as well as biological and chemical weapons of mass destruction, are now available to almost all challengers of the status quo who have the will to use them.

It is absurd at this late date to go on pretending that, because no commando units or hit teams of powerful revolutionary organizations or "potential adversaries" have actually seized any nuclear plant for terrorist purposes, the thing is unlikely or even impossible. If it starts to happen, it need not happen often to produce its most devastating effects. Those able to do such a thing will obviously not do it before they are prepared to carry through some overall design for our government's collapse. In March 1979 *U.S. News and World Report* published an article, prepared with full cooperation of Federal agencies, concerning what officials look upon as the "inevitability of terrorist attempts to go after nuclear bombs." In brief: "To these officials, it isn't a question of whether such an attack will be made but where and when."

Yet far more ominous was the article's acknowledgment that all current safeguard measures are based on the assumption that the attacking bands of terrorists would consist of fifteen members or less. All the safeguards currently ordered (though by no means effectively implemented) become irrelevant, one highly competent official said, if you assume that the goal of terrorists is not to blow up a city but to use the nuclear weapon for high-stakes political blackmail.

The question inevitably poses itself: What is to be done? There is no mystery about it. The book-length (661-page) report of the National Advisory Committee on Criminal Justice Standards and Goals, issued on March 2, 1977, at one point addresses the question quite unambiguously. In stressing the mounting threat of high technology terrorism, they recommended that every state should have the power to pass legislation rapidly to deal with emergency situations.

What the report urged most stringently, however, was that law enforcement agencies be given specific power to gather intelligence on individuals and groups that "might become involved" in technological violence. The point was that, if a terrorist group were preparing to fabricate nuclear weapons from stolen materials, as of now officials would not know about it until it was too late. A good start had been made on the gathering of such intelligence and the maintenance of computerized files on suspects or possible

suspects; but since Watergate and all the investigatory
attacks on the CIA and FBI, that has become at most non-
existent. Yet, in the words of the 1977 report, it is "unques-
tionably necessary" that law-enforcement agencies be given
the power, under specific legislation, to carry out covert
activity "designed to combat the activities, the organization, or the existence of those against whom they are
directed."

Reason of State or Media-Morality

More particularly still, the report urged that, under
conditions of emergency, authorized police power should
include "the power of search without warrant of persons
and property," the power to "enter premises by force and
without warrant," and the right to detain people without
arresting them. It further stressed that law-enforcement
personnel who happened to exceed their emergency powers should not be held personally liable, either criminally
or civilly, for any harm stemming from their behavior. The
relative quiet of the recent past, it warned, "is a false calm,
and we must see in [it] an accumulation of trouble for the
future."

Although he had not originally ordered it, James
Earl Carter was the President who received the National
Advisory Commission's report. On March 10, 1977 — a few
days after the report was released — the matter came up at
a presidential news conference. One reporter, in the guise
of asking a question, made a kind of brief and highly loaded
speech in which he challenged the President to say, on the
spot, whether he favored "certain recommendations of the
commission." Taking the matter completely out of context, as if it were some up-dated version of the Nixon Re-
election Campaign Committee schemes for dealing with
White House-lawn protestors, the reporter said : "Well, sir,
in the report there were certain recommendations such as
the use of mass arrests, the use of preventive detention,
some of the very things that were used in the sixties and

later ruled inappropriate in the courts, and I wondered, sir, what you felt about this problem involving human rights in the United States."

Had he not been a first-term President seeking his party's nomination for a possible second term, Mr. Carter might have responded differently than he actually did. He might conceivably have taken his cue from one of our more eminent retired ambassadors and former governors, ably representing the traditions of an old New England family — John Davis Lodge — who, in a recent letter to the *New York Times,* drew on his long experience in revolutionary trouble-spots of Europe and South America to urge that, for its own domestic good, our government should discipline itself to become "more geopolitical and less evangelical" in its conduct of foreign policy. And then, drawing the domestic lesson, he concluded:

> If we could stop preaching, we might even be able to learn something from our friends in Argentina, Uruguay, and Chile regarding how they have successfully handled and are handling the most cunning, cynical, vicious, brutal, relentless challenge of our time. When will we catch on that the ideological conflict is taking place in a jungle world? . . . In Argentina, Chile, Paraguay, Bolivia, and in Brazil they have sought the confrontation out of which victory has gradually emerged. The security forces are prevailing against the imperialistic drive from Moscow via Havana. In the countries of Western Europe, the will to resist, sapped by years of war, has been further eroded by chicanery and by raw terrorism . . . . The contrast between the healthy zest for the struggle in South America and the decadent defeatism rampant in Western Europe is dramatic.

Instead of the counsels of tough ex-ambassadors or tough national advisory commissions, what a first term President seeking re-election is most inclined to heed, it seems, is the advice of election-ad men who now look upon TV night-show hosts as the models of how a first-term President ought to look and talk if he hopes to have an "extended run" hosting the White-House show. The rule is: Don't be *heavy,* or the relaxing bedroom audience will "switch off." How did the President feel about the hard and heavy recommendations of the Advisory Commission for equipping ourselves to face the challenge of revolutionary terrorism? Approximating the tone of a successful night-show host, Mr, Carter said:

> I would be opposed to mass arrests and I would be op-posed to preventive detention as a general policy and even as a specific policy unless it was an extreme case. Obviously in a 600-page report there would be things with which we would agree and things with which we would disagree. I've not seen the report. I'm not familiar with it. But I think that the abuses, in the past have in many cases exacerbated the disharmonies that brought about demonstrations. And I think that the arrest of large numbers of people without warrant or preventive detention is contrary to our own best system of govern-ment.

Conclusion

On the basis of the depressing chronicle presented here about our governmental handling of threats of nuclear terrorism in the late 1970s, it is clear that what has so far most characterized the members of our ruling elites, with very few exceptions, is a total lack of even the beginnings of an adequate response. It is our firm prediction that nothing significant will be done (barring a wholesale turn-over or "circulation" of elites) until the things that threaten have actually occurred, perhaps several times. Then, in an atmosphere of chaos, everyone will be willing to accede to the very ugliest of totalitarian governments, if it will only stop the horrors and restore order.

To avoid a collapse into the chaos of a technologi-cally-terrorized extreme state of democratic indecision, for which the only cure conceivable would be a totally despotic government we need to consider and discuss publicly, with greater seriousness than ever before, the requirements of what the ancients used to call "constitutional dictatorship" or, preferably, constitutionally-defined and constitutionally-limited "crisis government." Since the days of our tragic Civil War, many distinguished American scholars and statesmen, some of whom ought to become better known than they are, have made significant contributions to the subject, both in word and deed.

Let me merely point in conclusion to Professor Arthur S. Miller's chapter on the emergency powers of Presidents — outside of declared war — in his finely-reasoned book *Presidential Power* (West Law School series, 1977). "Reason of state," he there concludes, "has always been, is, and will continue to be a thread running through the living constitution . . . . The problem [for America] now is how to live with the emergency power, for the citizenry are going to have it whatever they may wish and whatever the constitution implies."

8. THE URBAN-GUERRILLA THREAT

From all recent reports, it appears that the American strategy for containing revolutionary violence at home parallels the strategy of limited war we have pursued abroad since 1961. Drew Middleton of the *New York Times* noted the parallel recently in an article where he describes and analyzes current Western political-military thinking on the threat of urban guerrilla warfare. If his information is accurate — and we have no reason to suppose that it is not, since he quotes generously from the U.S. Army field manual and similar sources from other Western countries — then the politically determined U.S. military strategy and tactics themselves constitute one of the gravest of all threats to American national security.

All Western military authorities admit, Middleton relates, that the guerrilla is abandoning his traditional locales. From his mountain fastnesses and jungle retreats, he is moving into the "asphalt jungle." It is recognized, moreover, that urban-based guerrilla groups in various nations have established a communications network, and can shift arms and specialists about as needed.

What plans does our government have to counter this threat? The strategic principle that now guides our military thinking, Middleton stresses, is restraint — at all costs, restraint. Local police must meet any revolutionary thrust first. If they fail, state police may be called in; then national guardsmen, and finally, and only as a last resort, federal troops. On each level, moreover, the principle remains the same: restraint at all costs.

That is the opposite of the traditional strategy governing external wars. On this point, Middleton quotes Brigadier C. N. Barclay. Barclay notes that, while the object of external war has traditionally been to inflict the maximum number of casualties, in internal war "the rule is to use the minimum force consistent with the attainment of the object — the restoration of law and order on the spot." The American army field manual insists on the same distinction. The idea seems to be that, if overwhelming force is used initially, public sympathy may be aroused for the guerrillas. Another assumption, dubious at best, must be that a well-equipped military establishment can afford to hold back, confident that it can easily bring overwhelming force to bear when necessary.

What that last assumption overlooks is the capacity of revolutionaries to immobilize and secure defections in the military as disturbances are under way. In one of the most widely circulated communist manuals on the subject, *Armed Insurrection*, we read, for instance:

> The history of all revolutions shows that if an army and police force with good military training, provided with every modern technique of attack and defence . . . with good commanders, and supported by the armed fascist detachments which exist in every country today, fight effectively against the revolution, they are capable of rendering the latter's victory singularly difficult, even if all other conditions are favorable. In all past insurrections without exception, the decisive role has always been played by the army. . . . For the passage of power from one class into the hands of another class is ultimately decided by material strength. And the army is the key element of that strength.

Until an army's discipline is subverted, its force on the government's side is too much for the revolutionaries to cope with. But subversion is always possible. Marxist cadres work hard at it — helped by the fact that, in our case, Calleys are tried as war criminals, General Lavelles are demoted for fighting to win, and Al Haigs (favored by our Kissingers) are raised in less than three years from Colonel to four-star general. Our army could destroy North Vietnam in an afternoon. Yet it has been ordered to lose that war. Is it destined to face final defeat in the streets of our own cities? *Armed Insurrection* concludes:

> The entire experience of past revolutions shows that the conquest of the troops will be achieved in the actual course of the fighting, through direct contact between the revolutionary masses and the wavering elements of the army, who are already demoralized. This will be the physical struggle for the army of which Lenin speaks, involving extermination of the officers.

Professor Crane Brinton of Harvard has covered the same ground in his modern classic, *The Anatomy of Revolution*. Early in every revolution, he says, there is always "a point, or several points, where constituted authority is challenged by the illegal acts of revolutionists." The routine response of all governments in such instances is "to have recourse to force, police or military." In all the revolutionary situations studied by Professor Brinton, the governing authorities made such a response, "*but in each case with a striking lack of success.* Those of the ruling class responsible for such responses proved signally unable to make adequate use of force."

That is the American situation today — but certainly not the Soviet or Israeli or South African situation. Of Moscow's way of coping with civil disorders, Middleton writes: "Students of Soviet tactics that were used in crushing uprisings in Eastern Europe say that the Russians believe that law and order are restored fastest by the application of maximum force." In Czechoslovakia in 1968, for example, where maximum. force was used at once, "resistance incidents, although well publicized in the West, were infrequent." The consequence, ironically, was that fewer persons died and less blood was shed than would have been the case had the seemingly more humanitarian American approach of restraint at all costs been applied.

American "gradualism" in timidly meeting unpleasant necessities, as in Vietnam and the Attica prison [riot], is what sends causalities sky high. It is the false charity of cowardice. The great African Bishop, St. Augustine, made the point back in the 5th century in discussing true almsgiving:

> The man who corrects with blows, or restrains by any kind of discipline one over whom he has power, and who at the same time forgives from the heart the sin by which he was also injured, and prays that it may be forgiven, is also a giver of alms. (*Enchiridon*, LXXII)

It is because it is inspired by the false humanitarianism of cowardice that our current law-and-order policy is doomed to fail. In his "literary gospel of revolutionary syndicalism," *Reflections on Violence*, Georges Sorel remarked that the decisive factor on the eve of revolution will always be "the cowardice of the government." Governmental cowardice encourages dissent to become resistance and resistance to become armed insurrection. It is impossible to respect a cowardly government. And so the revolutionary contagion spreads, to the right as well as to the left. Ordinary citizens become astonished, Sorel continues, at the "timidity of the forces of law and order in the presence of a riot." They see that their governors, mayors, police commissioners, and other magistrates "who have the right to demand the services of soldiers dare not use their power to the utmost, and officers allow themselves to be abused and struck with a patience hitherto unknown to them." From that moment on it's a down-hill course.

Our military know better ways of dealing with riots. But they are under the "civilian control" of a class of politicians which is itself in the snares of the self-styled conscience elite that runs our universities and news-media. Whatever its ultimate motives, that elite makes cowards of us all. And our influence contaminates the entire West.

In England and France, too, it is clearly the politicians who have failed the military. For political reasons, De Gaulle's France surrendered its governance of Algeria (not to the original Berbers, of course, but to the Arabs who

followed the old Romans as invaders). But at least until the
political surrender, the French army on the spot com-
ported itself effectively. General Jacques Massu, Commander of French paratroops in Algiers, for instance, was
never compelled to start slow and exercise restraint at all
costs. In his book, *La vrai bataille d'Aiger* (Paris, 1972), he
sums up and justifies morally his strategy for handling
urban guerrillas. That strategy is analyzed also in Robert
Moss' *Urban Guerrillas: The New Fate of Political Violence*
(London, 1972), where its success is contrasted with the
failure of British strategy in Cyprus. According to Moss,
the Cyprus terrorists were militarily ineffective. They succeeded nevertheless because the British government let
itself be infected by a "withdrawal psychology" (like ours in
Vietnam), which inhibited it from taking the necessary
decisive countermeasures that less moralistic governments
would have used to stamp out the terrorist movement
overnight.

In contrast, General Massu (to whom Mr. Moss is
not at all sympathetic) dealt most decisively with the terrorists of Algiers. To find them out, he built up an effective
intelligence network, mainly by the systematic use of torture. As the beleaguered Israelis have so often successfully
done, he also enforced the principle of collective responsibility, by making individuals responsible not only for the
good behavior of their families, but for whole streets and
neighborhoods. Massu was thus able to smash the Algiers
terrorist organization in two months.

Torture as a means of maintaining order is an awful
thing. For James Beckett (author of *Barbarism in Greece*),
who recently discussed it in a *New York Times* article, it is
"the ultimate corruption, the grossest denial of man's
humanity, and its use never justified." Yet, of its effectiveness, he says:

> Those who condemn torture on political grounds, "there
> are better ways to get information," miss the major
> political use, which is not to gain information, but to

neutralize the majority of the population. If the state sets torture as the price of dissent, the rulers can be assured that only a small minority will react. This minority can then be isolated and the repressive power of the state concentrated on it.

On this point the lessons of history are clear. Faced with armed terrorist insurrection, a threatened government must either respond decisively with force, or perish.

As the revolutionary messianic movements daily grow less fearful and more powerful, and wend their seemingly inexorable course to the final confrontation (abdication would be more accurate term), the American conservative leaders who once talked frankly and fiercely against dangers far less imminent suddenly appear to have nothing to say. Can it be that they are too busy playing softball with the Javitses, or dining with the Lowensteins, or chatting with the Abbie Hoffmanns about LSD In Miami Beach hotels, or simply shilling for place and patronage at the New Nixon's old politics-as-usual convention?

America needs a new coalition of patriots if it is to survive. The mass base for the coalition has always been present, in the patriotism of the American working classes which, with minor exceptions, have always preferred national honor (not to be confused with corporation profits or vote-buying welfare subsidies) to their economic self-interest. To that base must be added the potential political force of our loyal police and military who, at least temporarily, must boldly take initiative in the public arena. They must not be denied, or deny themselves, an active role in our political process now that almost all other government employees and dependants — ranging from welfare workers and their clients up to Supreme Court Justices — make no scruple of using their positions to foster "social change" through "creative disorder."

But, if the new coalition is to be truly worthy of America's origins and promise, it must also be joined by that saving remnant of a patriotic intellectual elite — I think of the William Randall Elliotts, the Charles Burton Marshalls, the Herbert Deanes, and scores of others — which has always been in our midst but has heretofore disdained to make its presence fully felt politically on the side of popular patriotism.

9. TERRORISM AND THE MEDIA

In the wake of the [Patricia] Hearst and Murphy terrorist kidnappings, various types of experts (government officials, political scientists, psychologists, etc.) have warned that we may be in for a wave of similar brutal incidents in the immediate future. At the outset of such a trend — assuming the predictions to be correct — it is advisable to analyse and clarify the strategies and above all the interests of the various parties involved.

Among the major interests that have already surfaced in the Hearst case, several are clearly in conflict, because of their divergent goals. There is first of all the interest of the victim and her loved-ones, which, under painful constraint, tends to identify itself, unfortunately, with the kidnappers' interest, at least until the victim has been safely returned. Superficially in conflict with both of these (while they tend thus to be identified) is the "public interest," as represented by the law-enforcing agencies. Hanging heavily over the whole business there is, finally, the interest of the vast communications-industry which, as it makes money by mongering news, cannot for long resist sensationalizing a "good story." The added dimension here is that we are faced with a *terrorist* kidnapping, not merely a money-making crime; and that is the dimension that must finally concentrate our attention if our analysis of conflicting interests is to be politically meaningful.

Reportedly it was a local news story about the fabulous size of the Hearst "capitalist empire" that prompted the Symbionese Liberation Army terrorists to plot this "anti-capitalist" kidnapping. The University of California's student directory provided Patricia Hearst's address. The terrorists then proceeded, on the pattern of our popular novels and films, to break into her apartment and seize her. The *New York Times* has thus defined the "Army's" objectives: "The motive for this abduction appears to be two-fold: to bring the organization to national attention and to make the point that the left is now ready to use terror to achieve its professed goals."

Surely, with the help of the press and the conduct of the Hearst family, these two terrorist goals have been conspicuously well achieved. Randolph Hearst has made it plain that, to secure his daughter's safe return, he is prepared to sacrifice as much of his wealth as he can; and that, so far as honor goes, he is apparently ready — as a symbol of American capitalism — to kneel in abject degradation before the "misguided idealists" who have abducted his daughter, with millions in his outstretched hands, to plead and grovel, and take their contemptuous spittle in his face, if need be. Can that lesson be lost on anyone?

But Hearst and his family would apparently sacrifice much more than what belongs to them alone, if permitted to do so. The attitude is one with which we can easily sympathize, given the circumstances. Yet there are grave dangers for our nation in it. Mr. Hearst was reported by the *Times* as having "understood" that "his daughter's well-being was uppermost in the minds of the police agencies." That might have seemed harmless enough. But later, after the Attorney General issued his mild statement about "enforcing the laws," Hearst hastened to say that he "did not think Mr. Saxbe 'is in a position to have an opinion'."

What is at issue here is the nature of the public interest in a terrorist kidnapping. Clearly, Mr. Saxbe, as the chief legal officer of the United States, *is* in a position to have an opinion — in a position, indeed, that *requires* him to have an opinion. The federal law he is charged to administer provides for the safety not of any one person but of the nation as a whole. And similarly the police agencies within our system of law enforcement should *not* have the safety of Patricia Hearst "uppermost" in their minds, but rather the safety of the entire nation. Thus there is, on the surface, a conflict of family interest and public interest in this case, with responsible officials charged to secure the public interest at all costs — which is to say, at the expense, if necessary, of the private interest. Such interests are by no means necessarily in conflict and, in the long run, among persons educated to the responsibilities as well as to the privileges of free citizenship, they become wholly and unmistakably complementary. Yet when misfortune strikes a family, there is an understandable concern not to make any precipitous and perhaps needless sacrifice of the private interest.

Plato, at the very dawn of Western philosophic thought, drew emphatic attention to this problem. He set it down as one of the great practical principles of his *Republic* that, in order to secure a just social order, members of the ruling elite should not be allowed to have wives or families. This prohibition was needed, he reasoned, because of the natural tendency and danger that the immediate individual and familial interest would be preferred to the common interest of all the other individuals and families in the political system.

While many of us would not accept Plato's drastic solution, the problem is certainly well-enough defined in his pages. Pursuing a similar line of thought, Aristotle, St. Thomas Aquinas, and Abe Lincoln all agree that while a limb is justly sacrificed to save a body, a body is never wisely sacrificed or even endangered to preserve a limb. Even the left-leaning authors of the novel *Fail-Safe* advance the same principle by having their Kennedy-like President order the dropping of an atomic bomb on New York City, while his family is there, rather than risk an all-out nuclear war with the Soviet Union.

Beyond the interests of the Hearst family, of the kidnappers, and of the law-enforcing agencies, there looms, as we said, the interest of the news media — symbolically and effectively represented by the *New York Times*. Its first

editorial intervention in the Hearst case (Feb. 9) was an
anguished wringing of hands, followed by what sounded
like a call for a nation-wide witch hunt. "Society has the
urgent obligation," it thundered angrily, "to search out
these insane ones in its midst and put them where they are
beyond the possibility of doing further harm."

Two weeks later, however, the *Times* reversed itself.
On February 23, 1974, it joined Mr. Hearst editorially in
castigating Attorney General Saxbe for his "position" on
law enforcement, and went on to praise F.B.I. Director
Kelley (who persists in handling the affair as just another
criminal kidnapping) for his position that the safe return of
the victim dominates the bureau's actions.

"The first priority," said the *Times* editorial, "must
go to saving innocent lives." Enforcing the law is virtually
meaningless in such cases since, as everyone knows, persons who do such things are by definition insane, crazed,
demented, etc.; besides which, terrorism's irrationality
reveals itself unmistakably — so the *Times* concludes — in
the fact that it "usually has little or no relationship to the
culpability or authority of the particular victim."

The *Times* thus reveals its abysmal ignorance, or
pretended ignorance, of the coldly calculating rational
strategies of our contemporary leftist terrorists. One avowed
terrorist strategy is that violence be directed — rationally,
not irrationally — against the innocent in society. Why? To
produce general and widespread fear and insecurity so that
people at large will lose confidence in their government's
competence, or even willingness, to protect them. A second avowed terrorist strategy moves from the opposite
perspective, directing its violence against the most visible
manifestations of what it calls the "corrupt capitalist order." By striking at government buildings, army camps,
banks, and individual capitalists at the nation's nerve
centers, it can hope that one day the entire body can all of
a sudden be immobilized. Unlike the *Times'* editorial writ-
ers, its noted columnist C. L. Sulzberger is admittedly well-

informed on the rationality of terrorist strategies. In writing about the assassination of the American Ambassador to the Sudan, Sulzberger quoted Carlos Marighella's *Minimanual of the Urban Guerilla,* where terrorist strategies and tactics are spelled out with terrifying rationality. Sulzberger, at any rate, was moved by it to suggest the "possibly retrograde step" of reinstituting the death penalty for terrorists, if for no other reason than to reduce the number of convicted terrorists held in prisons, since a major cause of terrorist actions is to free imprisoned terrorists.

But what specifically is the news-media interest in the Hearst case? Is it perhaps a 1930s-type concern to sound an alarm, to get the public stirred up so as to root out a public danger before too much harm is done? Is it, as recently alleged, to secure the safety of the innocent victim? Or does it have a distinctly fourth-estate interest that is wholly self-serving, and therefore potentially in conflict with both the Hearst interest and the public interest, though not with the Symbionese Liberation Army interest — which is also, at least for the moment, in the news-making business.

By no means do we suggest that the conscience-stricken *Times* willfully abets terrorist movements. No. As Marighella, Bayo-Giraud, Guillen, and other strategists counsel, terrorists must make indirect use of the media. Given the "first-amendment" claims of our major TV networks and papers like the *Times,* this is relatively easy to accomplish. *Laissez-faire,* long since dead as a principle in American capitalist enterprise, now reigns unchallenged in such news centers, which, by a kind of divine right, claim absolute freedom to publish what they will, and absolute secrecy in regard to sources. One part of this bundle of absolute rights brings the media into conflict with Mr. Hearst; the other brings it into conflict with the national interest.

Here's the record. On February 20, while Mr. Hearst was trying to meet the monetary demands of the SLA, the

Times ran a news column revealing the contents of an IRS report that showed a Hearst portfolio of stock valued at $74 million. A *Times* representative personally examined the report; but it was later taken from him, as the *Times* informs us all, including the SLA, because "it was feared "a disclosure of the assets would not be in the public interest, considering that Miss Hearst is held by a group that has made ransom demands for her release." Yet the *Times* made the disclosure. And the SLA obviously took note of it.

On Feb. 23, when the Hearst family and the Hearst Foundation spokesman offered $4 million ransom as an absolute maximum, another *Times* story revealed that "two foundations established by the Hearst family had resources of more than 45 million." In the same edition, black correspondent Earl Caldwell (of shield law fame} provided a long backgrounder on the SLA. He cited "informed sources," a prominent "member of the group," etc. Can police agencies question Mr. Caldwell? Well, of course not! It would be a violation of the confidentiality of sources.

Finally, the obvious conflict between both private and national interest on the one hand and media interest on the other is evident in regard to the amount of publicity given the case. Terrorists depend — their strategists emphasize — upon the prominence given their action by the presspeople, who do so in the interest of such "bourgeois propaganda" values as the public's right to know. We are all aware that the enormous TV and press publicity given this SLA kidnapping is likely to stimulate other terrorist groups, and less rational persons, to imitate what was successfully done here. A most absurd incongruity appeared, however, on CBS-TV News (New York City edition) on February 22, 1974. CBS, apparently beguiled by the *Times* into accepting the insanity theory of terrorism, duly sent out one of its sweet young feminine things to interview a psychologist. The latter, needless to say, confirmed the insanity theory of terrorism. But he also remarked authoritatively that most of our terrorists seem to be motivated primarily by imitation and a craving for publicity. If so, then CBS obviously should never have telecast the interview at such length, or given such widespread publicity to the story in its news. Yet it did. *Fiat veritas, pereat mundus.*

Popular literature also has its comparable effect in liberal western societies. Simply by reading that best-selling "anti-Nazi" novel the *Odessa File,* we can learn in precise detail how to construct a bomb to blow up a car from materials purchased at any shopping-center. At least two lesser known novels have been cited as models for the Hearst operations. But "freedom of the press" hangs on through it all.

The relation between terrorist actions and media coverage is, however, complex and reflexive. As a *Times* staffer pointed out in a Sunday edition several weeks ago, the media tires of the mundane, the usual. Thus in order for another terrorist organization, or the same one, to receive the same amount of publicity — which is the first purpose of terrorist action — it must exceed the previous ones in either violence or sensationalism. Without overtaxing the imagination, might we not be justified in visualizing the following scenario for the near future?-

The next-of-kin of the heads of major capitalist and news-media enterprises — Exxon, IBM, CBS, *Times, Post,* with possibly *National Review* added, just to be "fair" — are seized. Perhaps one at a time; perhaps several at a time. But to catch and hold the media, there will have to be *new twists.* Why not, to begin with, reduce monetary demands (since money is what capitalists hold most dear) and intensify the attacks on honor (since that's what capitalists lack)? Perhaps the corporate heads might be forced to hand out food packages themselves, rather than through faceless functionaries, and at their own medieval exurbanite estates — with private transportation provided to get the "poor" out there.

Why not require further that each of these notables (as penance for his "crimes" against humanity, etc.) make a public show of his new-found contempt of self by licking the feet, or kissing the backside, of each recipient of a food package? If TV and the press should threaten rashly not to cover the "event," they would of course be made to realize that they have thereby assumed direct responsibility for the deaths that are certain to follow upon such failure to cooperate.

Is that too far-fetched? Perhaps only after something of this sort has actually happened can this nation get on with the business of seriously repressing elitist terrorism. Perhaps then the national interest will no longer be defecated upon for the sake of private, group, or media interests. Or, as the latest folk-hero of the Western liberal press, A. Solzhenitsyn, correctly advised on the Op-Ed page of the *Times* (9/15/73): "As soon as firmness is shown, terrorism can be smashed forever. Just remember that."

10. CRISIS GOVERNMENT AS A PROBLEM IN PUBLIC ADMINISTRATION: F. M. WATKINS AND EMERGENCY POWERS

Frederick M. Watkins, for many years a professor and department chairman in politics and government at Yale University and a well known writer, published at the outset of World War II *The Failure of the Constitutional Emergency Powers under the German Republic* (1939) — one of his lesser works but perhaps of far greater significance than some of his major studies, especially today, as we teeter on the edge of chaos through those crisis with which we have all grown familiar, and in particular, the possibility of a terrorist-induced crisis of mega-death proportions. His central argument in that detailed and well-documented study was that constitutional emergency powers (principally Article 48 of the Weimar Constitution) failed not because they allowed for the transference of too much power to the executive and thereby permitted a Hitler to seize power. Rather, they failed to allow for *enough* power to be granted to the executive; and the powers that were granted were too hemmed in with various restrictions and too much legislative oversight. Those excessively democratic impediments crippled the executive in his attempts to handle the economic crisis and the various communist and national socialist armed insurrections and *thereby* allowed Hitler to seize power. Had not Germany had even such a weak version of crisis government, Watkins argues, Hitler (or someone very like him) would have seized power much earlier. Only because of Article 48 was the advent of the Nazi regime delayed as long as it was. This analysis is, of course, in direct contravention to the prevailing popular and academic liberal wisdom that it was Article 48 that

conveniently allowed Hitler to seize power clothed in the
garb of constitutionalism.

But Carl J. Friedrich also agreed with Watkins on
this matter. In *Constitutional Government and Dictatorship*
(4th ed., 1968, Ch. XXV, "Constitutional Dictatorship and
Emergency Powers," p. 563), Friedrich wrote:

> The ill-famed Article 48 of the Weimar constitution was
> not nearly as noxious as legend has made it. One tends
> to forget that without it the first president of that
> republic might not have been able to master the emer-
> gencies of the first few years, more especially those of
> 1923. What was bad about Article 48 lay beyond that
> article, in the misconstrued dualism of presidential and
> chancellorian power which led to the second presiden-
> tial term of the aged Hindenberg.

Watkins's volume of 1939 was a detailed case study.
It is, however, his much shorter, generalizing study of the
same problem in a later article that provides us at once with
a more extensive analysis and an historical account of the
development of the institution of crisis government. The
occasion was the first issue of *Public Policy* (1940), published by Harvard's Graduate School of Public Administration, to which Watkins contributed a fifty-four page article
(pp. 324-379) on "The Problem of Constitutional Dictatorship. "

The Problem Defined

Watkins begins by posing the question: "Can dictatorship be made to serve the ends of constitutional government?" Anticipating the inevitable criticism from his liberal colleagues that the temporary use of dictatorship in
the interest of preserving a democratic nation will result in
long-range damage to the democratic character of the
system, Watkins bluntly observes:

> When a man is trying to save himself from falling off a
> stepladder, he is not likely to give much thought to the
> dangers of overexertion. When a social group is faced

with an immediate threat to its existence, it also cannot afford to calculate in terms of a very distant future. Whatever its ultimate advantages may be, there are times when constitutionalism can no longer be tolerated as a basis for political organization. In the face of pressing dangers, any question as to the long-run consequences of absolutism becomes purely academic. There is no point in worrying about the future unless you are sure that you have a future to worry about.

Moreover, Watkins continues, since decades and generations are needed for the development of constitutional government, it is only the recently established one that is more likely to be destroyed, because of its fragility, by even a short period of emergency government. In contrast, a long-established one, such as the United States or Great Britain, can sustain an emergency government for much longer periods, even years, without very great danger to its basic constitutionalism.

Watkins lists three basic criteria which distinguish constitutional dictatorship from other forms of absolutism:

1. It will be just sufficiently absolute to safeguard the interests of the established constitutional order.
2. It will continue in existence only so long as those interests are actually in danger.
3. And it will be followed by an integral return to the previous constitutional order.

But to demand perfection in regard to these criteria, he maintains, would be to set up a wholly false standard of judgment. Just as the idea of a circle is not to be discarded merely because it is impossible to make a perfectly circular object, so too the institution of constitutional dictatorship should not be discarded merely because the limitations on it cannot be perfectly established. The real question, Watkins emphasizes, "is whether it can be approached within useful limits of approximation." In fact, "gross inadequacy in the face of unusual situations has been found in practice to be a good deal more damaging than flexibility as a threat to the prestige of established institutions."

On the basis of manifest necessity, Watkins points out, some form of dispensing power has found a place in all legal systems. The problem of constitutional dictatorship is only a special instance of this more general problem. In more familiar areas of law, he notes, emergency action is quite accepted as a matter of course. We have, for example, chief executives issuing pardons for individuals, or even amnesties for large numbers of people. Such actions set aside the normal course of the law. When such analogous problems are being solved every day in these other areas of legal action, Watkins remarks, it is then difficult to believe that constitutional principles alone are not capable of achieving the necessary flexibility in the face of emergency needs. But from the standpoint of practical politics, the real problem of constitutional dictatorship is to establish conditions that tend to lessen the destructive effect of temporary absolutism. The most important condition is that the period of dictatorship must be relatively short. Reiterating his earlier point, Watkins maintains that "in regions where those usages are firmly established, a dictatorial interlude might last perhaps for several years without disastrous consequences."

A second major condition is that dictatorship should always be strictly legitimate in character. In regard to the United States now, some forty years after Watkins wrote, there remains a major question concerning this condition. The basic law governing it is the National Emergencies Act of 1976 [amplified by Congressional action after September 14th, 2001]. It is thus certainly legal. But as to whether those enormous grants of power which the President is authorized to wield under the terms of that act are constitutional is quite another matter. The constitution, it is generally agreed, does not provide for emergency powers other than for the suspension of *habeas corpus*. Both Rositer in *Constitutional Dictatorship* and Arthur Miller of Harvard Law School in *Presidential Power* argue that it is and has been throughout American history unconstitutional — albeit necessary; but that it should be put into the constitution, for, in the words of Miller, the American people are going to have it whether they like it or not.

Watkins's last condition for its success is that final authority to determine the need for dictatorship in any given case must never rest with the dictator himself. This condition is established by the act of 1976. Although initial prerogative to declare an emergency is there given to the President, final authority does rest with Congress, since it can overrule him.

Administrative Prerogatives and Legislative Restraints

But the problem of constitutional dictatorship, Watkins explains, involves two things: not just the problem of power, but also the problem of its limitations. The first requires sufficient extraordinary power and the second entails an effective external check on that power. Watkins at once admits that the two "are to some extent mutually inconsistent. If the discretion of a dictator were limited at all points by subservience to a higher authority, he would cease for all practical purposes to have any value as an independent agent, and his power would be inadequate even to the simplest emergency needs." But above all, the example of ancient Rome — "a fully constitutional state," and "the most strikingly successful of all known systems of emergency government" — "shows that an effective working compromise is by no means beyond the bounds of possibility. Through a wise combination of imperfectly compatible elements, the problem of constitutional dictatorship can be solved within useful limits of approximation."

The two principal modern versions are the state of siege and martial rule. In his discussion of these models,

Watkins observes that few people are aware of the extent
to which liberal countries have been willing to go in this
direction. "But the fact is that a distinct need for constitutional dictatorship . . . is common to all constitutional
systems." In contrast to the widespread impression, modern emergency systems "tend to be rather more extreme
than the dictatorship of ancient Rome." In the modern
period, the main problem of constitutional dictatorship is
to increase the effectiveness of executive action. The main
task of it is therefore to provide freedom in the realm of
administration. "For the sake of convenience, this may be
defined as the problem of administrative dictatorship."

In modern times, Watkins continues, the need for
administrative dictatorship has been recognized in all
constitutional states:

> Nowhere, indeed, are the underlying uniformities of
> political liberalism more strikingly apparent than in
> connection with the problem of constitutional dictator-
> ship. Superficially there is a good deal of difference
> among the various constitutional states of modern times.
> Some are monarchies and others republics. Some are
> federal, others unitary states. Some follow the presiden-
> tial, others the parliamentary pattern of executive re-
> sponsibility . . . . But in their treatment of the problem
> of administrative dictatorship all these countries are
> characterized by a considerable degree of basic agree-
> ment.

In civil law countries, the principal legal basis for
constitutional dictatorship is provided by the state of siege.
In liberal constitutional governments, the main checks on
administrative action are to be found in the bill of rights,
in the independence of the judiciary, and in the principle
of federalism. The function of the state of siege is to
remove the more irksome of the restraints in the periods of
foreign invasion or of armed insurrection. The second
main consequence of the state of siege, according to
Watkins, is to transfer all powers relative to the mainte-

nance of public order from the civil to the military authorities. Since federalism breaks up the unity of administrative action by guaranteeing a certain area of independence to local agencies of government, the transfer of political functions from the civil to the military authorities has a distinctly centralizing effect. "The third great consequence" of the state of siege is to relieve the administration from restraints normally imposed by an independent judiciary: the regular courts are automatically deprived of their competence to deal with offences against the public order, which are assigned to special military tribunals acting under particularly summary rules of procedure.

In common law countries, as Watkins describes in detail, similar results are achieved through the use of martial rule. Although it is characterized by a considerable degree of vagueness, martial rule is "nothing more than a special application of the general common law principle that, whenever the reign of law is interrupted by a display of illegal force, it is the duty of all citizens, including government officials, to take all necessary steps for the restoration of legitimate authority. 'Reasonable necessity' is the only recognized test for determining the legitimacy of actions taken on this basis." However, under the common law, no attempt is made to specify those rights which must be suspended. "This leads on occasion to measures of extreme consequence."

On martial law in the United States, Watkins significantly cites the famous case of Moyer v. Peabody in which "no less celebrated a liberal than Mr. Justice Holmes declared that 'when it comes to a decision by the head of the State upon a matter involving its life, the ordinary rights of individuals must yield to what he deems the necessities of the moment.'"

Watkins concludes that "so far as the extent of emergency authority is concerned, therefore, the institutions of modern administrative dictatorship leave little or nothing to be desired."

But Watkins sees the reverse tendency present in regard to legislative dictatorship — dictatorship which allows the executive to legislate. He speaks of "an extreme desire" evident in "modern liberal constitutions" to "safeguard the position of parliamentary bodies" by striking out emergency legislation entirely "from the list of executive prerogatives." That has been in sharp contrast, he notes, with the "casual irresponsibility of those same liberals in their dealings with administrative dictatorship." In fact, however, their sudden "access of caution" in this regard hasn't really deterred administrative dictatorships from straying into the "forbidden preserves" of legislation, when that has seemed attractive or necessary. Summing up his appraisal of the institutions of both administrative and legislative dictatorship, as modern liberal constitution-makers have tended to conceive them, Watkins concludes:

> We have seen that the powers granted are in some respects inadequate. In the face of this inadequacy, what services are they capable of rendering to the cause of political liberalism? We have also seen that these same powers are in many cases insufficiently safeguarded against the danger of abuse. How serious is the resulting threat to the maintenance of liberal institutions? These are the complex and conflicting factors which would have to be weighed in reaching any true estimate as to the significance of modern constitutional dictatorship.

Of course, from our post-Watergate perspective, it is obviously no longer true to say with Watkins:

> So far as administrative dictatorship is concerned, we have seen that the modern tendency, if anything, has been toward excessive prodigality in ascribing emergency prerogatives to the executive. Even in liberal states the tradition of a highly centralized executive is so strong that the prospect of temporary administrative despotism is greeted with relative indifference.

That was in 1940, when the American liberal intelligentsia was eager to enhance the powers of the New Deal Presidency. Today, the exact reverse is true. Despite his full consciousness of being the nation's first non-elected, interregnum chief executive, even Gerald Ford felt he could not sign the post-Watergate National Emergencies Act without a demurrer that it was in important respects an unconstitutional congressional infringement on presidential power.

The Ideological Impediment: Elitist Failure of Nerve

But the main problem of constitutional dictatorship is not, as Watkins describes it, constitutional-legal. The main problem was when he wrote, as it indeed is now, ideological. In popular democratic culture and among the academic, political, ecclesiastical, and media elites, the authoritarian measures sanctioned by a crisis government are felt to be incompatible with and utterly antithetical to a democratic system. The main administrative problem is thus far more one of securing ideological acceptance than it is one of the proper technical rubrics of administering such a system. Clinton L. Rossiter, in a brief preface to the 1963 edition of his seminal work on the subject, *Constitutional Dictatorship: Crisis Government in Modern Democracies* (1st publ. 1948), after having weathered the ideological broadsides of his liberal colleagues, more than hinted at this problem:

> No one could be more aware than I of its [the book's] limitations and faults. The obvious of the former is that it makes too much of the law and too little of the sociology and psychology of crisis government; the most unsettling of the latter is the confusion I seem to have caused with my too ready assumption that "constitutional dictatorship" had been granted a secure place in the vocabulary of political science as the generic label for such government. That it has not been granted this place is a collective decision that I can protest but not alter. It is therefore likely that, if I had it to do all over again, I would replace the title of this book with the subtitle and restrict the application of "constitutional dictatorship"

to those venerable but still lively institutions of martial
rule, the state of siege, and martial law. When this book
first appeared, it was subjected to a great deal of valid
criticism by many scholars who had bothered to read it
and to a small volley of abuse by a few polemicists who
had not. I hope that all those who buy it in this . . . edition
will do me the favor of reading it, and will read it as the
work of a political scientist who is wholeheartedly committed to the principles, practices, and purposes of
constitutional democracy.

It seems advisable to mention briefly the basic
political tenets of Professor Watkins, lest he too be dis-
missed out of hand as a crypto-fascist or something or
other of that nature. In *The Political Tradition of the West,*
Watkins unequivocally equates all that is good in Western
civilization with liberalism. Thus liberalism "is the modern
embodiment of all the characteristic traditions of Western
politics. If liberalism fails to survive, it will mean the end of
the Western political tradition." (p. ix) "Modern liberalism
believes that freedom under the law is the proper condit
ion of man, and that the maintenance of that freedom
depends on the subordination of government officials to
the dictates of independently organized agencies of public
opinion. In one form or another these beliefs have always
been the characteristic assumptions of Western politics."
(p. x)

But at the very end of this panegyric of liberalism,
Watkins (writing in 1948) warns his liberal colleagues and
the political elites of his day:

If liberal statesmen fail in the near future to satisfy the
prevailing hunger for economic and military security,
the masses of mankind will turn with relief to the apparent simplicity and certainty of dictatorial solutions . . . .
Liberalism offers the one last chance to preserve the
characteristic achievements of Western civilization for
the benefit of future generations.

It would be hard to find a more emphatic justification of

both constitutional dictatorship and of liberalism.

Still, like Rossiter, Watkins too despairs of breaking through the ideological mindset of his liberal colleagues. In the article in *Public Policy* he suggests that perhaps we should invent an entirely new term for the institution, to make a kind of end run around the liberal mindset, by adopting one "that is new and relatively unspoiled." But after a brief discussion, he too sees no solution to the problem. The resistance is clearly to the thing — to the very idea of constitutional self-preservation at all cost — not to the names under which it periodically presents itself for discussion.

The Trump Card or "Final Solution"

Yet is it conceivable that our modern liberal constitution-makers would admit of no *other* recourse in dealing with the institutional crises of liberal democracy in our time than the sort of constitutional administrative dictatorship that Watkins proposes? Well, not exactly. It appears that their despair is limited quite narrowly to nation-based remedies. Typical in this regard is the national gloom and supranational optimism of Brian Jenkins of the Rand Corporation. Jenkins is perhaps the most frequently cited expert dealing with technological terrorism, particularly of the nuclear variety. A glance at the titles of his publications on the subject, dating from 1975, gives us fresh insight into the general reluctance to deal with the problem on a "merely national" scale. His pamphlet of 1975 titled "Will Terrorists Go Nuclear?" was followed by "Terrorism and the Nuclear Safeguards Issue" (1976), "The Potential for Nuclear Terrorism" (1977), and "The Consequences of Nuclear Terrorism" (August, 1979). Then in September 1979 came a monograph with the interesting title (emphasis added) *"When* Terrorists 'Go Nuclear' . . . . A Look at the Consequences for World Order."* As the Rand advertisement explains:

Terrorist bombings, assassinations, kidnappings, and

hijackings have become part of our daily news diet. But what if we woke up one morning to find that terrorists were holding an entire city hostage with a stolen or clandestinely fabricated nuclear weapon? Such speculation is hardly idle, according to author Brian Jenkins, who has written extensively for Rand for the past five years on the subject. Analysis ranges over the types of increased security and surveillance at nuclear facilities that would result and the public policy issues governments would have to face: increasingly harsh measures against dissidents; the possibility of pre-emptive strikes against terrorist groups and even other states which may be proven to have aided or abetted terrorist groups; perhaps even the surrender, voluntarily or involuntarily, of the notion of national sovereignty as we know it in favor of international control over national nuclear facilities.

The Rand flyer then quotes Jenkins himself: "A world in which nuclear terrorism has become a reality is inevitably an increasingly authoritarian world," and one in which there would be a strong "corresponding inclination toward, 'gun-boating' on the part of the most frequently targeted nations." The Rand flyer notes that this paper was "written for a special colloquium on the consequences of nuclear proliferation, sponsored jointly by the Central Intelligence Agency and the Department of Defense."

What the non-ideological political scientist must ask himself is which solution would be more onerous from the standpoint of democratic civil liberties, Watkins's crisis government or Jenkins's "involuntary" surrender of "national sovereignty as we know it."

To the ideologue, of course, crisis government, even when established in the democratic constitution, is despotic. And world government, established by forced surrender of national sovereignty, is democratic. The former receives the most virulent barbs from the tergamants of liberalism and libertarianism. The latter is viewed with the highest esteem by the Kantian-Kissingerians.

11. CONCLUSION: HIGH STAKES IN PRESIDENTIAL ELECTIONS

Risks of a Divided Electorate

That transfer of the Presidency of the United States with its incalculable powers should still be effected by popular vote is the most impressive political fact of our time. Even when the power was relatively insignificant, foreign observers marveled that we dared to risk popular election. Alexis De Tocqueville saw the campaigns of the 1830s as periods of national crisis, with people sharply divided against themselves, and the conduct of public affairs virtually paralyzed for the duration of the campaigns.

The question asked was why our Presidency hadn't undergone a transformation similar to that of the First French Republic, which had had a chief executive somewhat like ours, but which in less than three decades passed from limited-term elective status to appointment for life, to hereditary succession? DeTocqueville's answer was that, despite the sweeping powers assigned to it by the Constitution, the office was, in effect, "weak and circumscribed." In his judgment, no presidential aspirant had as yet aroused "the dangerous enthusiasm or the passionate sympathies of the people in his favor, for the simple reason that, when he is at the head of the government, he has but little power, little wealth, and little glory to share among his friends." But De Tocqueville foresaw that if ever the Union were to face a perpetual threat to its existence, the executive branch of government would inevitably assume an increased importance. It remained to be seen, then, whether it could still risk popular elections, which would become dangerous "in proportion to the internal embarrassments and external dangers of the country."

De Tocqueville wrote those words in 1835. For internal embarrassments today, read violence in the cities, drugs in the schools, streets and boardrooms, and scandals in the highest offices of our land. For dangers, read four decades of aggressive communism, the Gulf War, Haiti, and Bosnia. Our cities are in strife and our enemies want to bury us, but we still don't inherit presidents. We still divide and choose, for what we have inherited instead is a constitutional obligation to run risks, even in the atomic age. But things have changed in risk-taking. A man elected to the presidency these days can do a lot for the countless partisans who have swarmed around him during the campaign. In like manner, there is a lot that partisan factions can do for a candidate. If the circumstances are right and they press a hard bargain, partisan factions today can make a presidential aspirant come begging — especially an incumbent seeking re-election. And particularly should he find that, in trying to work up an electoral majority, he has run a little short, he will have to pay dearly for the marginal votes they are able to deliver. Individuals may escape the pressures by withdrawing from the race or by providing funding of their own, as some have done in recent years, but once the candidates have been nominated, nothing short of a political *coup d'etat* can prevent the hard-bargaining factions from mongering their votes and exacting the highest possible price.

Ideological Leverage

Since the time of our first presidential elections, the power, wealth and glory of the office have grown. However it is still true that what a President can actually do *in office,* as Chief Executive, is far less than what he can *propose to do* as a *candidate.* So long as a nation like ours holds together, defending itself and directing its progress toward self-appointed goals, the course it can follow will depend less on the moralizing proposals of the election campaigns than on the force of its basic, year-round, life-sustaining activities. The physical building up of the nation, the exploitation of its natural resources for food, clothing, and shelter, the organization of its manpower for industrial, commercial, professional, and bureaucratic enterprise, the provisions for education, transportation, and entertainment, as well as protection of lives and limbs — all these activities, in their cumulative effects, are like vectors in the composition of a single effective force. Diverse and complex as they may be in themselves, the basic productive, protective, and directive activities of the nation inevitably converge on one another. And the resultant is the course of the nation's development. A candidate wooing a factional minority may promise to set the nation's course arbitrarily, according to the indications of an ideological compass; and the promise may gain him the election. But if the ideological indications are too far out of line with the reality of forces, the factional minority is bound to be disappointed. It may be, for instance, that Woodrow Wilson could not have won in 1916 without the votes that came to him because of his professed determination to keep us out of war, or that Lyndon Johnson could not have won in 1964 had he not proposed to follow the foreign policy designs of the internationalist liberal intelligentsia which would otherwise not have supported him. But after the elections, in 1965 as in 1917, ideology simply had to give way before the general convergence of basic forces.

Since the end of World War II, we have heard a lot about presidential powers and leadership, and most of what has been said and written has been aimed at freeing the office from the pressures that have traditionally acted on it. The object has been to enable the President to keep the promises made during the campaign, even if they were promises made to an ideological minority. In other words, if, as a candidate, the President had made a public choice favoring one proposed course of action over another, and that choice has served to attract the support of an ideological faction, there ought to be a way for him, in office, to get the thing done. The meaning is clear: a President who has set a new course according to the indications of an ideological compass should not be crippled by an unenlightened Congress; a President who has had the benefit of the counsel of an intellectual minority should not have to suffer under the checks and balances of legislators who respect the interests of their constituencies.

But how much power do these special interest groups actually wield when it comes to influencing the policies demanded by the national forces acting on the office of the presidency? Can our militant "one-worlders," the anti-national forces so prevalent among academe, high finance and the media really influence what is the first and foremost duty of a chief executive: "to preserve, protect, and defend" the sovereignty of our national union? If we examine the events around President Lyndon Johnson's first solo election bid in 1964 and his decision to withdraw from any re-election in 1968, we can get a good idea of the tremendous power in the hands of a small minority of our citizens and begin to recognize their determination to follow their agenda for world government and world peace regardless of the cost to our institutions.

Johnson and Vietnam: Panic of the Doves

Upon his entry to the presidency, Lyndon Baines Johnson, first Southern President since the Civil War, pledged himself to carry on the Kennedy program he had inherited. But for the intelligentsia who had so successfully engineered the "education" of JFK to the concept of world government, there was little comfort in the words of LBJ. This Texan was big and rough and had not studied at Harvard. What alone could make him educatable was his soaring ambition.

To be an effective national leader — which is to say, to win the presidential office on his own, after having served out his predecessor's term — Johnson had to hold on to as much of the Kennedy support as possible. Johnson knew that as the eleven months to election day in 1964 passed he would have to maneuver even more effectively than Kennedy had done, to win the internationalist liberal faction over to his support. And it was only with the greatest difficulty that he finally succeeded. Had the Republican Party nominated a Rockefeller rather than the conservative Goldwater, it is doubtful that Johnson could have managed the trick. The leaders of the intelligentsia placed little trust in the man. Even after one of its past national chairmen had gained a place as Johnson's running mate, the powerful ADA — Americans for Democratic Action — was embarrassed to support him. On October 11, 1964, The *New York Times* wrote a sympathetic account of the organization's predicament.

A painful embarrassment to most ADA officials is the turn-about the organization has had to make in its attitude toward Lyndon Baines Johnson. During his tenure as Senate Majority Leader, the ADA repeatedly criticized him for collaborating with the Republican administration to scuttle liberal legislation. In 1959, it rated him with a liberal score of only 58 percent, and Mr. Johnson responded by labeling the ADA, "one of those extreme groups."

In the Senate, the Texan could afford to talk that way. But in quest of victory in 1964, he willingly bargained with that "extreme group" for support, offering in return what amounted to a continuation of the mandate they had received to teach the lesson so candidly explained by Zbigniew Brzezinski and Samuel P. Huntington in their jointly authored book *Political Power: USA/U.S.S.R., Similarities. and Contrasts, Convergence or Evolution.* That lesson is clearly stated: "It takes a strong government to score diplomatic, political, and military successes in a cold war. It takes an even stronger one to negotiate détentes, to carry off retreats, and to survive reverses . . . . The American

government may well be strong enough *vis-à-vis* its enemies
to accomplish the former; it may not be strong enough vis-
à-vis its own people to accomplish the latter."

The ADA went all out for LBJ, or, rather, all out
against his opponent, whom it proceeded to brand as a war-
mongering, fascist racist. It seemed that Johnson had
passed the course. The professors' division of "Citizens for
Johnson and Humphrey" ran a full-page ad in the *New York
Times* and other papers declaring: "We believe Lyndon
Johnson will make a good president because he *is* a good
president . . . . In this nuclear age of anxiety, he can be
trusted to speak with restraint."

But it was not to be. In February 1965, the internationalist intelligentsia was shocked by the issuance of a
"White Paper" on Vietnam entitled "Aggression from the
North: The Record of North Vietnam's Campaign to Con-
quer South Vietnam." It outlined a new campaign to
increase the U.S. defensive response and "make attacks by
air." Whatever honeymoon there may have been was over.
The paper did not reassure internationalists, whose purpose had been to teach the American people to gain their
ends by "carrying off retreats and surviving reverses"
instead of by the old ways of scoring "diplomatic, political,
and military successes." It took some time for a general
recognition of the fact that the President was trying to
reverse the tables on his erstwhile supporters. How the
opposition of the liberal intelligentsia to Johnson built up
and finally resulted in forcing him to announce his decision not to run for re-election is a matter for the history
books.

All the wit and cleverness that was marshaled to give
him a landslide victory over Goldwater in 1964 was marshaled to "dump" the man and discredit his administration, even if the Democratic Party had to be wrecked by
minority leverage to do so, even if the presidency had to be
turned over for a time to so hated an enemy of liberalism
as Richard Nixon.

In the final showdown the high strategists of ideological leverage will not risk total defeat for their cause. They will be prepared to bargain themselves into a position of minority leverage with every conceivable candidate, to "educate him," if possible, before the election, but certainly to be there should he chance to win. Their motto is what it has always been for the highly maneuverable, hard-bargaining minority of liberal internationalists: *in utrumque paratus.*